Quick & Easy
Traditional Cakes

p

Contents

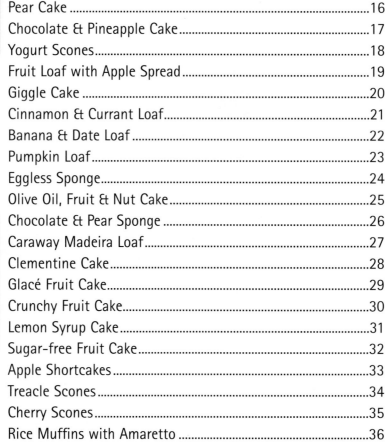

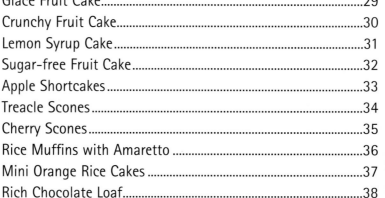

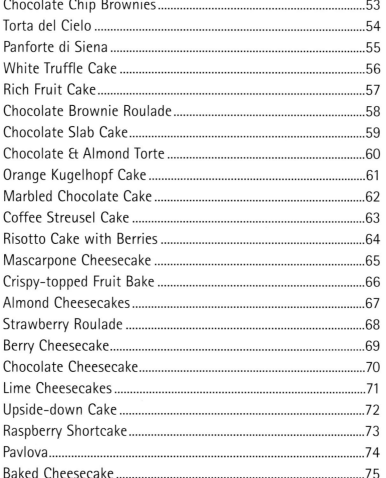

Introduction

Traditional cakes come in many varieties, from the homely and filling, made to be served as a snack with coffee or tea, or added to a packed lunch or a picnic, to the rich cake, impressive enough to be the centrepiece at a birthday party or an anniversary gathering, but which can double as a dessert for an evening meal. Every country has developed different traditions based on ingredients available locally - and cakes to go with them - and this book con tains many firm favourites. Supplementing these classics are new variations on their well-loved themes, plus some innovations.

Basic Ingredients

It is important to use the correct ingredients for cake-making and, where possible, to use the best quality in order to achieve the best results.

For cake-making you need mainly plain flour, or self-raising flour (which has a raising agent added). It is essential to use the type specified in the recipe. Do not be confused if a recipe calls for self-raising flour and a spoonful or two of raising agent.

White flour is used most often in cakes. Wholemeal flour is heavier and darker, and works well in fruit cakes. Both are available as plain or self-raising flours, and ground from organically grown wheat. Unbleached white flour may be used instead of bleached.

Caster sugar is finer than granulated sugar and is usually used in light cakes. Refined white sugar is commonly used, but unrefined golden caster sugar is also available and adds a richer colour and flavour to baking. For a rich, dark fruit cake or gingerbread, light or dark soft brown sugar is used. Sweetness can also be added in the form of honey - light and delicious, and a little less sweet than sugar - or treacle, thick and golden or black, and full of flavour

Butter is the fat that gives baking the best flavour, but polyunsaturated fat, in the form of margarine in block form or in a tub, can usually be substituted. It is also possible to make a fruit cake with olive oil, usually thought of as an ingredient in savoury foods.

A few recipes call for arborio rice - Italian risotto rice. Where it is specified it should be used in preference to a long-grain rice because when it is cooked it has a lovely creamy, almost sticky, texture.

Flavourings

A wide range of flavourings can be added to a basic cake mix to create something unusual. Vanilla is a classic ingredient to add to cakes, but be sure to use vanilla essence rather than vanilla flavouring. Alternatively, put a vanilla pod in a jar of caster sugar and leave it for a few weeks. It will take on the delicious, distinctive scent and flavour of the vanilla.

The finely grated rind of citrus fruits - lemon, orange or lime - gives a lovely fresh tang to sponge cakes, fruit cakes, roulades and creamy cheesecakes. Little bottles of citrus oils are also available as flavourings for baking.

The aroma of a spicy cake just baked is enticing, evocative and usually irresistible. Cinnamon, ginger and freshly grated nutmeg are the spices traditionally used in baking. Another classic is the caraway seed, whose aniseed flavour may be intriguingly difficult to identify in a buttery madeira cake.

Coffee adds a special richness to a cake. And at the top of the list of favourite cake flavourings is chocolate. It is used in the form of cocoa powder, top-quality chocolate with a high cocoa-butter content, chocolate chips, and chocolate essence. Sponge cakes, brownies,

roulades - there is plenty of scope for using chocolate.

Many fruits add flavour and texture to baking. Dried fruits, such as sultanas, raisins, dates and currants work well with mixed spice (a blend of cinnamon, coriander, nutmeg, cloves and ginger). Glacé fruits, moist and colourful, are popular, but cakes may also contain fresh fruits. Apples and pears, perhaps flavoured with cloves, make a delectable cake that may be served warm as a dessert with whipped cream or ice-ream; while banana cakes,

with their special aroma, are loved by children. Cranberries, fresh or dried, add a slightly tart flavour that offsets the sweetness of tea breads and muffins. Berries, such as raspberries and strawberries, are delicious in creamy cakes such as roulades, pavlovas, and cheesecakes.

Carrots are the best-known vegetable used in cakes and muffins, tinting them gold; but recipes also use pumpkins and potatoes to create a distinctive texture.

Coconuts and nuts are a must for the storecupboard. You need walnuts and hazelnuts, but most especially ground almonds, which have a natural sweetness and bring a touch of luxury to any cake recipe.

Basic cake-making

Most recipes follow a basic method of preparation. The most common are creaming and rubbing-in.

Creaming The fat and sugar are beaten together, either by hand with a wooden spoon, or with an electric whisk, until the mixture is pale and creamy; the eggs are then added a little at a time, then the flour is folded in with a metal spoon: the mixture is turned over lightly until all the ingredients are blended.

Rubbing-in This method is often used for fruit cakes or tea breads, and is similar to that used for making pastry. The fat is rubbed into the flour with the fingertips until it has the consistency of crumbs, then the sugar, eggs and other ingredients are added.

Muffins These are small cakes made by a fast and simple method. Dry ingredients (flour, sugar and seasonings) are put in a large bowl and wet ingredients (beaten eggs, milk and corn oil or butter) are mixed together and stirred into the dry ingredients until they are just combined. It is important not to over-stir.

Handy Hints

Cake-making is very easy as long as you observe a few rules regarding preparation:

1. Follow the recipe step by step, to be sure of obtaining the result you hope for.
2. Assemble all the ingredients needed before you begin to cook.
3. Set the oven on to heat to the temperature specified in the recipe. A fan-assisted oven may need a slightly lower temperature (and a shorter cooking time).
4. Prepare the baking tins. Always use the correct size and shape of tin as specified in the recipe, or your cake may bake very flat, or fail to cook all the way through. Grease

and line the tin if required to make it easier to turn out the cake. Paper cases are available for all sizes of tin, and are quicker to use than baking paper.
4. Weigh out all the ingredients, and bring items such as fat and eggs to room temperature.
5. Chop, grate, slice, and otherwise prepare any ingredients that need to be ready for mixing and blending when you begin following the recipe.
6. Check the cake towards the end of the specified cooking time. Sponge-type cakes and muffins are cooked if the mixture springs back when lightly touched. Heavier cakes are cooked when a skewer inserted into the centre comes out clean. Shortcake and scones are ready when they are slightly coloured on top.
7. Once the cake is out of the oven, cool it as instructed in the recipe. Some cakes can be left to cool in the tin, while others must be turned out onto a wire rack.
8. Most cakes are best stored in an airtight tin, but cakes containing cream or cheese should be kept in the refrigerator. Some cakes need to be left to mature for a few days or even weeks to develop their flavour. Wrap these in greaseproof paper to prevent them drying out.

KEY	
	Simplicity level 1 – 3 (1 easiest, 3 slightly harder)
	Preparation time
	Cooking time

Vanilla Tea Cake

Slices of juicy fruit soaked in sugar syrup are one of the great delicacies of Provence and southern Italy. They make a glorious flavouring for this cake.

NUTRITIONAL INFORMATION

Calories 264	Sugars 23g	
Protein 4g	Fat 15g	
Carbohydrate ...31g	Saturates 7g	

  30 mins   1½ hours

SERVES 4

INGREDIENTS

225 g/8 oz quality glacé fruit, such as cherries, and candied orange, lemon and lime peels

85 g/3 oz ground almonds

finely grated rind of ½ lemon

85 g/3 oz plain flour

85 g/3 oz self-raising flour

175 g/6 oz butter (softened), plus extra for greasing

175 g/6 oz plus 2 tbsp vanilla-flavoured sugar (see Cook's Tip)

½ tsp vanilla essence

3 large eggs, lightly beaten

pinch of salt

glacé fruit, to decorate

1 Grease a loaf tin (measuring approximately 22 x 12 x 5 cm/ 8½ x 4½ x 2 inches) with butter, then line the base of the tin with a piece of baking parchment.

2 Chop the fruit into uniform small pieces, reserving a few larger slices for the top. Place in a bowl with the ground almonds, lemon rind and 2 tablespoons of the measured plain flour and stir together. Set aside.

3 Beat the butter and flavoured sugar together until fluffy and creamy. Beat in the vanilla essence and eggs, a little at a time.

4 Sift both flours and the salt into the creamed mixture, then fold in. Fold in the fruit and ground almonds.

5 Spoon into the tin and smooth the surface. Arrange the reserved fruit on the top. Loosely cover the tin with kitchen foil, making sure it does not touch the cake mixture. Bake in a preheated oven at 180°C/350°F/ Gas Mark 4 for about 1½ hours until risen, and a skewer inserted into the centre comes out clean.

6 Cool in the tin on a wire rack for 5 minutes, then turn out and remove the lining. Cool completely on a wire rack. Wrap in kitchen foil and store in an airtight container for up to 4 days. Serve decorated with glacé fruit.

COOK'S TIP
Make your own vanilla-flavoured sugar by storing a sliced vanilla pod in a closed jar of caster sugar.

Italian Lemon Rice Cake

This lemon-flavoured cake should have a crisp crust with a soft, moist centre. Soaking the currants in rum brings out their flavour.

NUTRITIONAL INFORMATION

Calories 283	Sugars 24g	
Protein 7g	Fat 10g	
Carbohydrate . . .41g	Saturates 6g	

 1 hour   40 mins

SERVES 8–10

I N G R E D I E N T S

1 litre/1¾ pints milk

pinch of salt

200 g/7 oz arborio or pudding rice

1 vanilla pod (split), seeds removed and reserved

60 g/2¼ oz currants

50 ml/2 fl oz rum or water

2 tsp melted butter, for greasing

cornmeal or polenta, for dusting

140 g/5 oz caster sugar

grated rind of 1 large lemon

60 g/2¼ oz butter, diced

3 eggs

2–3 tbsp lemon juice (optional)

icing sugar

TO SERVE

175 g/6 oz mascarpone cheese

2 tbsp rum

2 tbsp whipping cream

1 Bring the milk to the boil in a heavy-based saucepan. Sprinkle in the salt and rice and bring back to the boil. Add the vanilla pod and seeds to the milk. Reduce the heat and simmer, partially covered, for about 30 minutes until the rice is tender and the milk is absorbed; stir occasionally.

2 Meanwhile, bring the currants and rum to the boil in a small saucepan; set aside until the rum is absorbed.

3 Take a cake tin (measuring 25 cm/10 inches) with a removable bottom, and brush the bottom and sides with butter. Dust with 2–3 tablespoons of cornmeal to coat evenly; shake out any excess.

4 Remove the rice from the heat and take out the vanilla pod. Add all but 1 tablespoon of sugar, plus the lemon rind and butter, and stir until the sugar is dissolved. Place in iced water to cool; stir in the currants and remaining rum.

5 Using an electric mixer, beat the eggs for about 2 minutes until they are light and foamy. Gradually beat in half the rice mixture, then stir in the rest. If using, stir in the lemon juice.

6 Pour into the prepared tin and smooth the top evenly. Sprinkle with the reserved tablespoon of sugar and bake in a preheated oven at 160°F/325°C/Gas Mark 3 for about 40 minutes until risen, golden and slightly firm. Cool in the tin on a wire rack.

7 Remove the cake from the tin and dust the top with icing sugar. Transfer the cake to a serving plate. Whisk the mascarpone with the rum and cream, and serve with the cake.

Spicy Carrot Rice Loaf

Rice flour gives this loaf a tender crumb while the rice adds a chewy texture. Use any kind of cooked rice – white, brown or wild.

NUTRITIONAL INFORMATION

Calories	330	Sugars	. . . . .27g
Protein	. . . . .5g	Fat	. . . . .12g
Carbohydrate	. . .53g	Saturates	. . . . . . .7g

 25 mins   1¼ hours

SERVES 8–10

INGREDIENTS

225 g/8 oz plain flour

85 g/3 oz rice flour

2 tsp baking powder

½ tsp bicarbonate of soda

½ tsp salt

1 tsp ground cinnamon

½ tsp ground nutmeg

½ tsp ground ginger

60 g/2¼ oz cooked risotto rice or long-grain white rice

60 g/2¼ oz pecan nuts, chopped

70 g/2½ oz sultanas or raisins

3 eggs

200 g/7 oz sugar

115 g/4 oz light brown sugar

115 g/4 oz butter, melted and cooled, plus extra for greasing

2 carrots, grated

icing sugar, for dusting

1 Lightly grease a loaf tin (measuring 23 x 13 cm/9 x 5 inches) with butter. Line the tin with non-stick baking parchment. Grease the parchment and dust lightly with plain flour. Preheat the oven to 180°C/350°F/ Gas Mark 4.

2 Sieve the flour, rice flour, baking powder, bicarbonate of soda, salt and spices into a bowl. Add the rice, nuts and sultanas and toss well to coat. Make a well in the centre of the dry ingredients and set aside.

3 Using an electric mixer, beat the eggs for about 2 minutes until light and foaming. Add the sugars and continue beating for a further 2 minutes. Beat in the butter by hand, then stir in the grated carrots until blended.

4 Pour the egg, sugar, butter and carrot mixture into the well in the dry ingredients and, using a fork, stir until a soft batter gradually forms. Do not over-mix – the batter should be slightly lumpy.

5 Pour into the prepared tin and smooth the top evenly with a knife. Bake in the oven at 180°C/350°F/Gas Mark 4 for 1–1¼ hours until risen and golden; cover the loaf with foil if it colours too quickly.

6 Cool the loaf in the tin on a wire rack for about 10 minutes. Carefully turn the loaf out and leave to cool completely. Dust the loaf with icing sugar and slice thinly to serve.

Pear & Ginger Cake

This deliciously buttery pear and ginger cake is ideal for tea time, or you can serve it with cream for a delicious dessert.

NUTRITIONAL INFORMATION

Calories	531	Sugars	........41g
Protein	.........6g	Fat	..........30g
Carbohydrate	...62g	Saturates	......19g

15 mins   40 mins

SERVES 6

INGREDIENTS

200 g/7 oz unsalted butter, softened, plus extra for greasing

175 g/6 oz caster sugar

175 g/6 oz self-raising flour, sieved

3 tsp ground ginger

3 eggs, beaten

450 g/1 lb eating pears, peeled, cored and thinly sliced

1 tbsp soft brown sugar

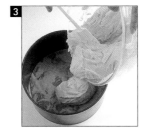

1 Lightly grease and line the base of a deep 20 cm/8 inch cake tin.

2 Using a whisk, combine 175 g/6 oz of the butter with the sugar, flour, ginger and eggs and mix to form a smooth consistency.

3 Spoon the cake mixture into the prepared tin, levelling the surface with a knife.

4 Arrange the pear slices over the cake mixture. Sprinkle with the brown sugar and dot with the remaining butter.

5 Bake in a preheated oven at 180°C/350°F/Gas Mark 4, for 35–40 minutes, or until the cake is golden and feels springy to the touch.

6 Serve the Pear and Ginger Cake warm, with ice cream or cream, if you wish.

COOK'S TIP

Soft brown sugar is often known as Barbados sugar. It is a darker form of light brown soft sugar.

Orange & Almond Cake

This light and tangy citrus cake from Sicily is better eaten as a dessert than as a cake. It is especially good served after a large meal.

NUTRITIONAL INFORMATION

Calories 399	Sugars 20g
Protein 8g	Fat 31g
Carbohydrate ...23g	Saturates 13g

30 mins   40 mins

SERVES 8

I N G R E D I E N T S

2 tsp melted butter, for greasing

4 eggs, separated

125 g/4 oz caster sugar, plus 2 tsp for the cream

finely grated rind and juice of 2 oranges

finely grated rind and juice of 1 lemon

125 g/4 oz ground almonds

25 g/1 oz self-raising flour

200 ml/7 fl oz whipping cream

1 tsp ground cinnamon

25 g/1 oz flaked almonds, toasted

icing sugar, to dust

1 Grease and line the base of a round, deep 18 cm/ 7 inch cake tin.

2 Blend the egg yolks with the sugar until the mixture is thick and creamy.

VARIATION

You could serve this cake with a syrup. Boil the juice and finely grated rind of 2 oranges, 75 g/ 2¾ oz caster sugar and 2 tbsp of water for 5–6 minutes until slightly thickened. Stir in 1 tablespoon of orange liqueur just before serving.

Whisk half the orange rind and all the lemon rind into the egg yolks.

3 Mix the juice from both the oranges and the lemon with the ground almonds, and stir into the egg yolks. The mixture will become quite runny at this point. Fold in the flour.

4 Whisk the egg whites until stiff and gently fold into the egg yolk mixture.

5 Pour the mixture into the cake tin and bake in a preheated oven, at 180°C/350°/Gas Mark 4, for about 35–40 minutes, or until golden and springy to the touch. Leave to cool in the tin for 10 minutes and then turn out. It is likely to sink slightly at this stage.

6 Whip the cream to form soft peaks. Stir in the remaining orange rind, cinnamon and sugar.

7 Once the cake has cooled completely, it can be decorated. Cover with the almonds, dust with icing sugar and serve with the flavoured cream.

Potato & Nutmeg Scones

Potato and nutmeg give these savoury cookies a different texture from traditional scones, and a subtle flavour.

NUTRITIONAL INFORMATION

Calories	178	Sugars 8g
Protein	.........4g	Fat 5g
Carbohydrate	...30g	Saturates 3g

30 mins   15 mins

SERVES 6

INGREDIENTS

2 tsp melted butter, for greasing

250 g/9 oz floury potatoes, diced

125 g/4¼ oz plain flour

1½ tsp baking powder

½ tsp grated nutmeg

50 g/1¾ oz sultanas

1 egg, beaten

50 ml/2 fl oz double cream

2 tsp light brown sugar, to decorate

1 Line a baking tray and lightly grease it with butter.

2 Cook the diced potatoes in a saucepan of boiling water for 10 minutes, or until soft. Drain thoroughly and mash the potatoes.

3 Transfer the mashed potatoes to a large mixing bowl and stir in the flour, baking powder and grated nutmeg, mixing well to combine.

4 Stir in the sultanas, beaten egg and cream, and then beat the mixture thoroughly with a spoon until it is completely smooth.

5 Shape the mixture into 8 rounds, 2 cm/¾ inch thick, and place on the baking tray.

6 Cook in a preheated oven, 200°C/ 400°F/Gas Mark 6, for about 15 minutes, or until the scones have risen and turned golden. Sprinkle with the sugar. The scones are delicious served warm and spread with butter.

COOK'S TIP

For extra convenience, make a batch of scones in advance and freeze them. Thaw thoroughly and when ready to serve, warm in a moderate oven.

Potato Muffins

These light-textured muffins rise like little soufflés in the oven and are best eaten warm. The dried fruit can be varied according to taste.

NUTRITIONAL INFORMATION

Calories 98   Sugars 11g
Protein ....3g   Fat 2g
Carbohydrate ...18g   Saturates 0.5g

  30 mins   20 mins

SERVES 4

I N G R E D I E N T S

4 tsp melted butter, for greasing

175 g/6 oz floury potatoes, diced

75 g/2¾ oz self-raising flour

2 tbsp soft light brown sugar

1 tsp baking powder

125 g/4 oz raisins

4 eggs, separated

1 Lightly grease 12 muffin tins with butter and dust with flour .

2 Cook the diced potatoes in a saucepan of boiling water for 10 minutes, or until tender. Drain well and mash until completely smooth.

3 Transfer the mashed potatoes to a mixing bowl and add the flour, sugar, baking powder, raisins and egg yolks. Stir well to mix thoroughly.

4 In a clean bowl, whisk the egg whites until standing in peaks. Using a metal spoon, gently fold them into the potato mixture until fully blended.

5 Divide the mixture between the prepared tins.

6 Cook in a preheated oven, 200°C/ 400°F/Gas Mark 6, for 10 minutes. Reduce the oven temperature to 160°C/ 325°F/Gas Mark 3 and cook the muffins for a further 7–10 minutes, or until risen.

7 Remove the muffins from the tins and serve warm.

COOK'S TIP

Instead of spreading the muffins with plain butter, serve them with cinnamon butter made by blending 60 g/2¼oz butter with a large pinch of ground cinnamon.

Banana & Lime Cake

A substantial cake, which is ideal served for tea. The mashed bananas help to keep the cake moist, and the lime icing gives it extra zing.

NUTRITIONAL INFORMATION

Calories 235	Sugars 31g
Protein 5g	Fat 1g
Carbohydrate ...55g	Saturates 0.3g

35 mins   45 mins

SERVES 10

INGREDIENTS

2 tsp melted butter, for greasing

300 g/10½ oz plain flour

1 tsp salt

1½ tsp baking powder

175 g/6 oz light muscovado sugar

1 tsp lime rind, grated

1 egg, beaten

1 banana, mashed with 1 tbsp lime juice

150 ml/5 fl oz low-fat fromage frais

115 g/4 oz sultanas

banana chips, to decorate

lime rind (finely grated), to decorate

TOPPING

115 g/4 oz icing sugar

1–2 tsp lime juice

½ tsp lime rind, finely grated

1 Preheat the oven to 180°C/350°F/ Gas Mark 4. Grease and then line a deep, round 18 cm/7 inch cake tin with baking parchment.

2 Sieve the flour, salt and baking powder into a mixing bowl and stir in the sugar and lime rind.

3 Make a well in the centre of the dry ingredients and add the egg, banana, fromage frais and sultanas. Mix well until thoroughly blended together.

4 Spoon into the tin and smooth the surface. Bake for 40–45 minutes until firm to the touch or a skewer inserted into the centre comes out clean. Cool for 10 minutes, then turn on to a wire rack.

5 To make the topping, sift the icing sugar into a small bowl and mix with the lime juice to form a soft, but not too runny, icing. Stir in the grated lime rind. Drizzle the icing over the cake, letting it run down the sides.

6 Decorate the cake with banana chips and lime rind. Let the cake stand for 15 minutes so that the icing sets.

VARIATION

For a delicious alternative, substitute orange rind and juice for the lime, and replace the sultanas with chopped apricots.

Blackberry & Apple Loaf

The sugar cubes give a lovely crunchy top to this moist bake, which makes the most of autumnal fruits.

NUTRITIONAL INFORMATION

Calories ....227 Sugars 30g
Protein ....5g Fat 1g
Carbohydrate ...53g Saturates 0.2g

🍰 30 mins   🕐 45 mins

SERVES 10

INGREDIENTS

2 tsp melted butter, for greasing

350 g/12 oz cooking apples

3 tbsp lemon juice

300 g/10½ oz self-raising wholemeal flour

½ tsp baking powder

1 tsp ground cinnamon, plus extra for dusting

175 g/6 oz light muscovado sugar

175 g/6 oz blackberries (prepared and thawed if frozen), plus extra to decorate

1 egg, beaten

200 ml/7 fl oz low-fat fromage frais

60 g/2¼ oz white or brown sugar cubes, lightly crushed

eating apple (sliced), to decorate

1 Grease and line a 900 g/2 lb loaf tin. Core, peel and finely dice the apples. Place them in a saucepan with the lemon juice, bring to the boil, cover and simmer for 10 minutes until soft and pulpy. Beat well and set aside to cool.

2 Sieve the flour, baking powder and cinnamon into a bowl, adding any husks that remain in the sieve. Stir in the sugar and 115 g/4 oz of the blackberries.

3 Make a well in the centre of the ingredients and add the egg, fromage frais and cooled apple purée. Mix well to incorporate thoroughly. Spoon the mixture into the prepared loaf tin and smooth over the top with a knife.

4 Sprinkle with the remaining blackberries, pressing them down into the cake mixture, and top with the crushed sugar cubes. Bake for about 40–45 minutes in an oven preheated to 190°C/375°F/Gas Mark 5. Leave the loaf to cool in the tin.

5 Remove the loaf from the tin and peel away the lining paper. Serve dusted with cinnamon and decorated with the extra blackberries and apple slices.

Carrot & Ginger Cake

This melt-in-the-mouth version of a cake whose popularity is international has a fraction of the fat of the traditional recipe.

NUTRITIONAL INFORMATION

Calories 249	Sugars 28g	
Protein 7g	Fat 6g	
Carbohydrate ...46g	Saturates 1g	

15 mins   1¼ hours

SERVES 10

INGREDIENTS

2 tsp melted butter, for greasing

225 g/8 oz plain flour

1 tsp baking powder

1 tsp bicarbonate of soda

2 tsp ground ginger

½ tsp salt

175 g/6 oz light muscovado sugar

225 g/8 oz carrots, grated

2 pieces stem ginger in syrup, drained and chopped

25 g/1 oz fresh root ginger, grated

60 g/2¼ oz seedless raisins

2 eggs, beaten

3 tbsp corn oil

juice of 1 medium orange

FROSTING

225 g/8 oz low-fat soft cheese

4 tbsp icing sugar

1 tsp vanilla essence

TO DECORATE

stem ginger

ground ginger

1 Preheat the oven to 180°C/350°F/ Gas Mark 4. Grease and then line a round 20 cm/8 inch cake tin with baking parchment.

2 Sift the flour, baking powder, bicarbonate of soda, ground ginger and salt into a bowl. Stir in the sugar, carrots, stem ginger, fresh ginger and raisins. Beat together the eggs, oil and orange juice, then pour into the bowl. Mix the ingredients together well.

3 Spoon the mixture into the cake tin and bake in the oven for 1–1¼ hours until firm to the touch, or test by inserting a skewer into the centre of the cake – if it comes out clean, the cake is cooked.

4 To make the frosting, place the soft cheese in a bowl and beat to soften. Sift in the icing sugar and add the vanilla essence. Mix well.

5 Remove the cake from the tin and smooth the frosting over the top. Decorate the cake and serve.

Pear Cake

This is a really moist cake, deliciously flavoured with chopped fresh pears, honey and ground cinnamon.

NUTRITIONAL INFORMATION

Calories 119	Sugars 16g
Protein 2g	Fat 0.3g
Carbohydrate . . .29g	Saturates 0g

40 mins   1½ hours

SERVES 4

I N G R E D I E N T S

2 tsp melted butter, for greasing

4 pears, peeled and cored

2 tbsp water

200 g/7 oz plain flour

2 tsp baking powder

100 g/3½ oz soft light brown sugar

4 tbsp milk

2 tbsp clear honey, plus extra to drizzle

2 tsp ground cinnamon

2 egg whites

1 Grease a 20-cm/8-inch cake tin and line the base.

2 Put 1 pear in a food processor with the water and blend until almost smooth. Transfer to a mixing bowl.

3 Sieve in the plain flour and baking powder. Beat in the sugar, milk, honey and cinnamon, and mix well.

4 Chop all but one of the remaining pears and add to the mixture.

5 Whisk the egg whites until they form peaks, and gently fold into the mixture until fully blended.

6 Slice the remaining pear and arrange the slices in a fan pattern on the base of the cake tin.

7 Spoon the cake mixture into the tin and cook in a preheated oven, at 150°C/300°F/Gas Mark 2, for 1¼–1½ hours or until cooked through (see Cook's Tip for how to test this).

8 Remove the cake from the oven and leave it to cool in the cake tin for 10 minutes.

9 Turn the cake out on to a wire cooling rack and drizzle the surface with honey. Leave to cool completely, then cut into slices to serve.

COOK'S TIP

To test if the cake is cooked through, insert a skewer into the centre – if it comes out clean, the cake is cooked. If not, return the cake to the oven and test at frequent intervals.

Chocolate & Pineapple Cake

Decorated with thick yogurt and canned pineapple, this is a low-fat cake, but it is by no means lacking in flavour.

NUTRITIONAL INFORMATION

Calories	199	Sugars	........19g
Protein	.........5g	Fat	...........9g
Carbohydrate	...28g	Saturates	......3g

 15 mins   25 mins

SERVES 9

I N G R E D I E N T S

2 tsp melted butter, for greasing

150 g/5½ oz low-fat (butter substitute) spread

125 g/4¼ oz caster sugar

100 g/3½ oz self-raising flour, sieved

3 tbsp cocoa powder, sieved

1½ tsp baking powder

2 eggs

225g/8 oz canned pineapple pieces in natural juice

125 ml/4 fl oz thick, low-fat natural yogurt

1 tbsp icing sugar

grated chocolate, to decorate

 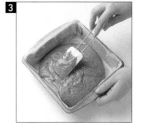 

1 Lightly grease a square 20 cm/8 inch cake tin.

2 Place the low-fat spread, caster sugar, flour, cocoa powder, baking powder and eggs in a large mixing bowl. Beat with a wooden spoon or electric whisk until smoothly blended.

3 Pour the cake mixture into the prepared cake tin and level the surface with a spatula or a palette knife. Bake in a preheated oven, 190°C/ 375°F/Gas Mark 5, for about 20–25 minutes or until springy to the touch. Leave the cake to cool slightly in the tin before transferring to a wire rack to cool completely.

4 Drain the pineapple, chop into pieces and then drain again. Reserve a little of the pineapple for decoration, then tip into a bowl. Stir in the yogurt and sweeten to taste with icing sugar.

5 Spread the pineapple and yogurt mixture over the top of the cake and decorate with the reserved pineapple pieces. Sprinkle with the grated chocolate before serving.

Yogurt Scones

Yogurt is a suitable alternative to buttermilk, providing just the acidity needed to produce perfect scones.

NUTRITIONAL INFORMATION

Calories 109	Sugars 5g
Protein 3g	Fat 4g
Carbohydrate . . .17g	Saturates 2g

15 mins   10 mins

SERVES 16

INGREDIENTS

225 g/8 oz flour, plus extra for dusting

1 tsp salt

1 tbsp baking powder

60 g/2¼ oz unsalted butter (chilled), plus extra for greasing

60 g/2¼ oz sugar

1 egg

6 tbsp low-fat natural yogurt

1 Sift together the flour, salt and baking powder. Cut the butter into small pieces, and rub it into the dry ingredients until the mixture resembles breadcrumbs. Stir in the sugar.

2 Beat together the egg and yogurt, and stir quickly into the dry ingredients. Mix to form a thick dough and knead until smooth.

3 Sprinkle flour on a pastry board or worktop and a rolling pin. Roll out the dough to a thickness of 1.5 cm/¾ inch.

4 Cut out rounds of dough with a 5 cm/2 inch pastry cutter, then gather up the trimmings, knead into a ball and roll out again. Cut out as many more rounds as possible.

5 Lightly grease a baking tray with butter and heat it in the oven. Transfer the dough rounds to the baking tray and dust lightly with flour.

6 Bake the scones in an oven preheated to 220°C/425°F/Gas Mark 7, for 10 minutes, or until they are well risen and golden brown. Cool on a wire rack.

VARIATION

For spiced scones, add up to 1½ teaspoons ground ginger or cinnamon to the flour.
For savoury scones, omit the sugar. At the end of step 1, stir in up to 45g/ 1½ oz grated mature Cheddar.

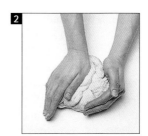

Fruit Loaf with Apple Spread

This sweet, fruity loaf is ideal served for tea or as a healthy snack.
The fruit spread can be made quickly while the cake is in the oven.

NUTRITIONAL INFORMATION

Calories	733	Sugars	.......110g
Protein	........12g	Fat	...........5g
Carbohydrate	...171g	Saturates	......1g

🔔 🔔 🔔

🍰 1½ hours   🕐 1½ hours

SERVES 4

INGREDIENTS

2 tsp melted butter, for greasing

175 g/6 oz porridge oats

100 g/3½ oz light muscovado sugar

1 tsp ground cinnamon

125 g/4½ oz sultanas

175 g/6 oz seedless raisins

2 tbsp malt extract

300 ml/10 fl oz unsweetened apple juice

175 g/6 oz self-raising wholemeal flour

1½ tsp baking powder

strawberries and apple wedges, to serve

FRUIT SPREAD

225 g/8 oz strawberries, washed and hulled

2 eating apples, cored, chopped and mixed
  with 1 tbsp lemon juice to
  prevent browning

300 ml/10 fl oz unsweetened apple juice

1 Preheat the oven to 180°C/350°F/ Gas Mark 4. Grease and line a 900 g/2 lb loaf tin.

2 Place the porridge oats, sugar, cinnamon, sultanas, raisins and malt extract in a mixing bowl. Pour in the apple juice, stir well and leave to soak for 30 minutes.

3 Sieve in the flour and baking powder, adding any husks that remain in the sieve, and fold in using a metal spoon.

4 Spoon the mixture into the prepared tin and bake for 1½ hours until firm, or until a skewer inserted into the centre comes out clean.

5 Leave for 10 minutes, then turn on to a wire rack and leave to cool.

6 Meanwhile, make the fruit spread. Place the strawberries and apples in a saucepan and pour in the apple juice. Bring to the boil, cover and simmer for 30 minutes. Beat the sauce well and spoon into a clean, warmed jar. Leave to cool, then seal and label.

7 Serve the loaf with 1–2 tablespoons of the fruit spread and an arrangement of strawberries and apple wedges.

Giggle Cake

It is a mystery how this cake got its name – perhaps the reason is because it is easy to make and fun to eat.

NUTRITIONAL INFORMATION

Calories 493	Sugars 66g	
Protein 6g	Fat 15g	
Carbohydrate ...90g	Saturates 3g	

25 mins   1 hour

SERVES 8

INGREDIENTS

2 tsp melted butter, for greasing

350 g/12 oz mixed dried fruit

125 g/4¼ oz butter or margarine

175 g/6 oz soft brown sugar

225 g/8 oz self-raising flour

pinch of salt

2 eggs, beaten

225 g/8 oz canned chopped
   pineapple, drained

125 g/4¼ oz glacé cherries, halved

1 Put the mixed dried fruit into a large bowl and cover with boiling water. Set aside to soak for 10–15 minutes, then drain well.

VARIATION

If you wish, add 1 teaspoon ground mixed spice to the cake mixture, sifting it in with the flour. Bake the cake in a round 18 cm/7 inch cake tin if you do not have a loaf tin of the right size. Grease and line it first.

2 Put the butter or margarine and sugar into a large saucepan and heat gently until melted. Add the drained dried fruit and cook over a low heat, stirring frequently, for 4–5 minutes. Remove from the heat and transfer to a mixing bowl. Set aside to cool.

3 Sift the flour and salt into the dried fruit mixture and stir well. Add the eggs, mixing until the ingredients are thoroughly blended together.

4 Add the pineapple and cherries to the cake mixture and stir to combine. Transfer to a greased and lined 1 kg/2 lb loaf tin and level the surface.

5 Bake the cake in a preheated oven, 180°C/ 350°F/Gas Mark 4, for about 1 hour. Test the cake with a fine skewer; if it comes out clean, the cake is cooked. If not, return to the oven for a few more minutes. Remove from the oven and allow to cool before serving.

Cinnamon & Currant Loaf

This spiced fruit tea bread is quick and easy to make. Serve it as an afternoon snack, buttered and drizzled lightly with honey.

NUTRITIONAL INFORMATION

Calories 439	Sugars 33g
Protein 7g	Fat 18g
Carbohydrate . . .67g	Saturates 11g

🍞 30 mins   🕐 1 hour 10 mins

SERVES 8

INGREDIENTS

150 g/5½ oz butter (chilled and cut into small pieces), plus extra for greasing

350 g/12 oz plain flour

pinch of salt

1 tbsp baking powder

1 tbsp ground cinnamon

125 g/4¼ oz soft brown sugar

175 g/6 oz currants

finely grated rind of 1 orange

5–6 tbsp orange juice

6 tbsp milk

2 eggs, beaten lightly

1 Grease a 900 g/2 lb loaf tin and line the base with baking parchment.

2 Sieve the flour, salt, baking powder and cinnamon into a bowl. Rub in the butter pieces with your fingers until the mixture resembles coarse breadcrumbs.

3 Stir in the sugar, currants and orange rind. Separately beat the orange juice, milk and eggs together, add to the dry ingredients, then mix well together.

4 Spoon the mixture into the prepared tin. Make a slight dip in the middle of the mixture to help it rise evenly.

5 Bake in a preheated oven, 180°C/ 350°F/Gas Mark 4, for about 1 hour up to 1 hour 10 minutes, or until a fine metal skewer inserted into the centre of the loaf comes out clean.

6 Leave the loaf to cool before turning out of the tin. Transfer to a wire rack and leave to cool completely before slicing and serving.

COOK'S TIP

Once you have added the liquid to the dry ingredients, work as quickly as possible because the baking powder is activated by the liquid.

Banana & Date Loaf

This tea bread, with its moist texture and rich flavour, is a popular classic, excellent for afternoon tea or coffee time.

NUTRITIONAL INFORMATION

Calories 432   Sugars 41g
Protein . . . . .7g   Fat 16g
Carbohydrate . . .70g   Saturates 10g

15 mins   1 hour

SERVES 6

INGREDIENTS

100 g/3½ oz butter (chilled and cut into
   small pieces), plus extra for greasing

225 g/8 oz self-raising flour

75 g/2¾ oz caster sugar

125 g/4¼ oz stoned dates, chopped

2 bananas, roughly mashed

2 eggs, lightly beaten

2 tbsp honey

1 Grease a 900 g/2 lb loaf tin and line the base with baking parchment.

2 Sieve the flour into a mixing bowl. Rub the butter into the flour with your fingertips, until the mixture resembles fine breadcrumbs.

3 Stir the sugar, chopped dates, bananas, beaten eggs and honey into the dry ingredients. Mix together to form a soft, dropping consistency.

4 Spoon the mixture into the prepared loaf tin and level the surface.

5 Bake in a preheated oven, 160°C/ 325°F/Gas Mark 3, for about 1 hour or until golden and a fine metal skewer inserted into the centre comes out clean.

6 Leave the loaf to cool in the tin before turning out and transferring to a wire rack to cool completely.

7 Serve the loaf warm or cold, cut into thick slices.

COOK'S TIP

This tea bread will keep for several days if stored in an airtight container and kept in a cool, dry place.

Pumpkin Loaf

The pumpkin purée in this loaf prevents it from becoming dry when baking. It is delicious eaten at any time of the day.

NUTRITIONAL INFORMATION

Calories 456	Sugars 33g	
Protein 7g	Fat 21g	
Carbohydrate ...62g	Saturates 12g	

 1¼ hours 2 hours 10 mins

SERVES 6

I N G R E D I E N T S

2 tsp vegetable oil, for greasing

450 g/1 lb pumpkin flesh

125 g/4¼ oz butter (softened), plus extra for greasing

175 g/6 oz caster sugar

2 eggs, beaten

225 g/8 oz plain flour, sieved

1½ tsp baking powder

½ tsp salt

1 tsp ground mixed spice

25 g/1 oz pumpkin seeds

1 Grease a 900 g/2 lb loaf tin with vegetable oil.

2 Chop the pumpkin flesh into large pieces and wrap in buttered kitchen foil. Bake in a preheated oven, 200°C/400°F/Gas Mark 6, for about 30–40 minutes until tender.

3 Leave the pumpkin to cool before mashing to a thick, creamy purée.

4 In a separate bowl, cream the butter and sugar together until they are a light and fluffy texture. Add the eggs a little at a time.

5 Stir in the purée. Fold in the flour, baking powder, salt and mixed spice.

6 Fold the pumpkin seeds gently into the loaf mixture. Spoon the mixture into the loaf tin.

7 Bake the Pumpkin Loaf in a preheated oven, at a temperature of 160°C/325°F/Gas Mark 3, for about 1¼–1½ hours, or test by inserting a skewer into the centre of the loaf – if comes out clean, the loaf is cooked.

8 Leave the loaf to cool and serve buttered, if wished.

COOK'S TIP

To ensure that the pumpkin purée is dry, place it in a saucepan over a medium heat for a few minutes, stirring frequently, until it is thick.

Eggless Sponge

This is a healthy variation of the classic Victoria sponge cake and because it contains no egg, it is suitable for vegans.

NUTRITIONAL INFORMATION

Calories 273	Sugars 27g
Protein 3g	Fat 9g
Carbohydrate . . .49g	Saturates 1g

20 mins   30 mins

1 x 8" CAKE

INGREDIENTS

2 tsp melted butter, for greasing

225 g/8 oz self-raising wholemeal flour

2 tsp baking powder

175 g/6 oz caster sugar

6 tbsp sunflower oil

250 ml/9 fl oz water

1 tsp vanilla essence

4 tbsp strawberry or raspberry reduced-sugar jam

caster sugar, for dusting

1 Grease two 20 cm/8 inch sandwich cake tins with butter and line them with baking parchment.

2 Sieve the self-raising flour and baking powder into a large mixing bowl, stirring in any husks remaining in the sieve. Stir in the caster sugar.

3 Pour in the sunflower oil, water and vanilla essence. Mix the ingredients thoroughly with a wooden spoon for about 1 minute until the mixture is completely smooth, then divide between the prepared tins.

4 Bake in an oven preheated to 180°C/350°F/Gas Mark 4, for about 25–30 minutes, until the centre springs back when touched lightly.

5 Leave the sponges to cool in the tins before turning out and transferring to a wire rack.

6 To serve, remove the baking parchment and place one sponge on a serving plate. Spread with the jam and place the other sponge on top.

7 Dust the Eggless Sponge with a small amount of caster sugar before slicing and serving.

Olive Oil, Fruit & Nut Cake

Use a good-quality olive oil for this cake, because the oil determines the cake's flavour. The cake will keep well in an airtight tin.

NUTRITIONAL INFORMATION

Calories 309	Sugars 17g
Protein 4g	Fat 17g
Carbohydrate ...38g	Saturates 3g

  20 mins   45 mins

SERVES 8

INGREDIENTS

2 tsp melted butter, for greasing

225 g/8 oz self-raising flour

50 g/1¾ oz caster sugar

125 ml/4 fl oz milk

4 tbsp orange juice

150 ml/5 fl oz olive oil

100 g/3½ oz mixed dried fruit

25 g/1 oz pine kernels

1 Grease an 18 cm/7 inch cake tin and line with baking parchment.

2 Sieve the flour into a mixing bowl and stir in the caster sugar.

3 Make a well in the centre of the dry ingredients and pour in the milk and orange juice. Stir the mixture with a wooden spoon, gradually beating in the flour and sugar.

4 Pour in the olive oil, stirring well so that all of the ingredients are thoroughly mixed.

5 Stir the mixed dried fruit and pine kernels into the mixture and spoon into the prepared tin. Smooth the top with a palette knife.

6 Bake in an oven preheated to 180°C/ 350°F/Gas Mark 4, for about 45 minutes, until the cake is golden and firm to the touch.

7 Leave the cake to cool in the tin for a few minutes before transferring to a wire rack to cool completely.

8 Serve the cake warm or cold, and cut it into long slices.

COOK'S TIP

Pine kernels are best known as an ingredient in the classic Italian pesto. Here they are used to give a delicate, slightly resinous flavour to this cake.

Chocolate & Pear Sponge

Fresh pear slices are placed on top of a chocolate sponge, making an ingenious combination of flavours for a dessert or a snack.

NUTRITIONAL INFORMATION

Calories 479	Sugars 24g	
Protein 7g	Fat 26g	
Carbohydrate ...57g	Saturates 16g	

30 mins   1 hour

SERVES 6

INGREDIENTS

175 g/6 oz butter, softened, plus extra for greasing

175 g/6 oz soft brown sugar

3 eggs, beaten

150 g/5½ oz self-raising flour

2 tbsp cocoa powder

2 tbsp milk

2 small pears, peeled, cored and sliced

1 Grease a 23 cm/8 inch loose-bottomed cake tin and line the base with baking parchment.

2 In a bowl, cream together the butter and soft brown sugar until the mixture is pale and fluffy.

3 Gradually add the beaten eggs to the creamed mixture, beating well after each addition.

4 Sieve the self-raising flour and cocoa powder into the creamed mixture, excluding any husks remaining in the sieve, then fold in gently until all of the ingredients are combined.

5 Gradually stir in the milk, then spoon the mixture into the prepared cake tin. Level the surface of the mixture with the back of a spoon or with a palette knife.

6 Lay the pear slices on top of the cake mixture, arranging them in a radiating pattern.

7 Bake in a preheated oven, 180°C/350°F/Gas Mark 4, for about 1 hour, until the cake is just firm to the touch.

8 Leave the cake to cool in the tin, then transfer to a wire rack to cool completely before serving.

COOK'S TIP

Serve the cake with melted chocolate drizzled over the top for a delicious dessert.

Caraway Madeira Loaf

This is a classic Madeira cake, made in the traditional way with caraway seeds. Plain versions, without the seeds, are also popular.

NUTRITIONAL INFORMATION

Calories 479	Sugars 24g
Protein 7g	Fat 26g
Carbohydrate ...57g	Saturates 16g

    30 mins   1 hour

SERVES 8

INGREDIENTS

225 g/8 oz butter (softened), plus extra for greasing

175 g/6 oz soft brown sugar

3 eggs, beaten

350 g/12 oz self-raising flour

1 tbsp caraway seeds

grated rind of 1 lemon

6 tbsp milk

1 or 2 strips of candied citron peel

 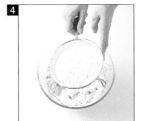 

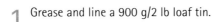

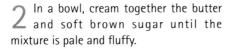

1 Grease and line a 900 g/2 lb loaf tin.

2 In a bowl, cream together the butter and soft brown sugar until the mixture is pale and fluffy.

3 Gradually add the beaten eggs to the creamed mixture, beating thoroughly after each addition.

4 Sieve the flour into the bowl and gently fold into the creamed mixture in a figure-of-eight movement.

5 Add the caraway seeds, lemon rind and the milk, and fold in until thoroughly blended.

6 Spoon the mixture into the prepared tin and level the surface.

7 Bake in a preheated oven at 160°C/325°F/Gas Mark 3 for 20 minutes.

8 Remove the Caraway Madeira Loaf from the oven, place the pieces of citron peel on top of it, and return it to the oven for a further 40 minutes, or until the loaf is well risen. Test by inserting a fine skewer into the centre – if it comes out clean, the loaf is cooked.

9 Leave the loaf to cool in the tin before turning out and transferring to a wire rack to cool completely. Serve in thin slices.

COOK'S TIP

Candied citron peel is available in the baking section of supermarkets. If it is unavailable, you can substitute chopped mixed peel.

Clementine Cake

This cake is flavoured with clementine rind and juice, filling its rich, buttery slices with a fresh fruit flavour.

NUTRITIONAL INFORMATION

Calories 427   Sugars 32g
Protein . . . . .6g   Fat 25g
Carbohydrate . . .48g   Saturates 13g

35 mins.   1 hour

SERVES 8

INGREDIENTS

175 g/6 oz butter (softened), plus extra for greasing

2 clementines

175 g/6 oz caster sugar

3 eggs, beaten

175 g/6 oz self-raising flour

3 tbsp ground almonds

3 tbsp single cream

GLAZE AND TOPPING

6 tbsp clementine juice

2 tbsp caster sugar

3 white sugar cubes, crushed

1 Grease a round 18 cm/7 inch cake tin with butter and line the base with baking parchment.

2 Pare the rind from the clementines and chop it finely. In a bowl, cream together the butter and sugar until pale and fluffy. Add the clementine rind.

3 Gradually add the beaten eggs to the mixture, beating thoroughly after each addition.

4 Gently fold in the self-raising flour, followed by the ground almonds and the single cream. Spoon the mixture into the prepared cake tin.

5 Bake in a preheated oven, 180°C/ 350°F/Gas Mark 4, for 55–60 minutes or until a fine skewer inserted into the centre comes out clean. Leave in the tin to cool a little.

6 Meanwhile, make the glaze for the cake. Pour the clementine juice into a small saucepan and add the caster sugar. Bring the mixture to the boil and simmer for 5 minutes.

7 Transfer the cake to a plate or wire rack. Drizzle the glaze over the cake until it has all been absorbed, and sprinkle with the crushed sugar cubes.

Glacé Fruit Cake

This cake is extremely colourful – you can choose any mixture of glacé fruits or stick to just one type if you prefer.

NUTRITIONAL INFORMATION

Calories 398	Sugars 34g	
Protein 5g	Fat 20g	
Carbohydrate . . .53g	Saturates 12g	

 25 mins   1 hour 10 mins

SERVES 8

INGREDIENTS

175 g/6 oz butter (softened), plus extra for greasing

175 g/6 oz caster sugar

3 eggs, beaten

175 g/6 oz self-raising flour, sieved

25 g/1 oz ground rice

finely grated rind of 1 lemon

4 tbsp lemon juice

125 g/4½ oz mixed glacé fruit, chopped

icing sugar, for dusting (optional)

1 Lightly grease an 18 cm/7 inch cake tin and line with baking parchment.

2 In a bowl, whisk together the butter and caster sugar until light and fluffy.

3 Add the beaten eggs, a little at a time, then fold in the flour and ground rice.

4 Add the grated lemon rind and lemon juice, followed by the chopped glacé fruits. Lightly mix all the ingredients together.

5 Carefully spoon the mixture into the prepared tin and then level the surface with the back of a spoon or palette knife.

6 Bake the cake in a preheated oven, 180°C/350°F/Gas Mark 4, for about 1 hour–1 hour 10 minutes, until well risen or until a fine skewer inserted into the centre of the cake comes out clean.

7 Leave the cake to cool in the tin for 5 minutes, then turn out on to a wire rack to cool completely.

8 Dust well with icing sugar, if using, before serving.

COOK'S TIP

Wash and dry the glacé fruit before chopping it. This will prevent it from sinking to the bottom of the cake during cooking.

Crunchy Fruit Cake

Polenta adds texture to this fruit cake, as well as a golden yellow colour. It also acts as a flour, binding the ingredients together.

NUTRITIONAL INFORMATION

Calories	...... .328	Sugars	........33g
Protein	........59g	Fat	..........15g
Carbohydrate	...47g	Saturates	.......7g

 30 mins   1 hour

SERVES 8

INGREDIENTS

100 g/3½ oz butter (softened), plus extra for greasing

100g/3½ oz caster sugar

2 eggs, beaten

50 g/1¾ oz self-raising flour, sieved

1 tsp baking powder

100 g/3½ oz polenta

225 g/8 oz mixed dried fruit

25 g/1 oz pine kernels

grated rind of 1 lemon

4 tbsp lemon juice

2 tbsp milk

1 Grease an 18 cm/7 inch cake tin with a little butter and line the base with baking parchment.

2 In a bowl, whisk together the butter and sugar until light and fluffy.

3 Whisk in the beaten eggs, a little at a time, whisking thoroughly after each addition.

4 Gently fold the flour, baking powder and polenta into the mixture and blend together well.

5 Stir in the mixed dried fruit, pine kernels, grated lemon rind, lemon juice and milk.

6 Spoon the mixture into the prepared tin and level the surface.

7 Bake the fruit cake in a preheated oven, 180°C/ 350°F/Gas Mark 4, for about 1 hour or until a fine skewer inserted into the centre of the cake comes out clean.

8 Leave the cake to cool in the tin before turning out.

VARIATION

To give a crumblier, lighter fruit cake, omit the polenta and use 150 g/ 5½ oz self-raising flour instead.

Lemon Syrup Cake

The lovely light and tangy flavour of the sponge is balanced by the lemon-flavoured syrup poured over the top of the cake.

NUTRITIONAL INFORMATION

Calories . . . . . . .424 Sugars 38g

Protein . . . . .6g Fat 21g

Carbohydrate . . .58g Saturates 5g

35 mins   1 hour

SERVES 8

INGREDIENTS

2 tsp melted butter, for greasing

200 g/7 oz plain flour

2 tsp baking powder

200 g/7 oz caster sugar

4 eggs

150 ml/5 fl oz soured cream

grated rind of 1 large lemon

4 tbsp lemon juice

150 ml/5 fl oz sunflower oil

SYRUP

4 tbsp icing sugar

3 tbsp lemon juice

1 Lightly grease a round 20 cm/8 inch loose-bottomed cake tin with melted butter and line the base with baking parchment.

2 Sieve the flour and baking powder into a mixing bowl and stir in the caster sugar.

3 In a separate bowl, whisk the eggs, soured cream, lemon rind, lemon juice and oil together.

4 Combine the egg mixture with the dry ingredients and mix thoroughly.

5 Pour the mixture into the prepared tin and bake in a preheated oven, 180°C/350°F/Gas Mark 4, for about 45–60 minutes until well risen and golden brown on top.

6 Meanwhile, to make the syrup, mix together the icing sugar and lemon juice in a small saucepan. Stir over a low heat until just beginning to bubble and turn syrupy.

7 As soon as the cake comes out of the oven, prick the surface with a fine skewer, then brush the syrup over the top.

Leave the cake in the tin to cool completely before turning out and serving.

COOK'S TIP

Pricking the surface of the hot cake with a skewer ensures that the syrup seeps right into the cake and the full flavour is absorbed.

Sugar-free Fruit Cake

The mixture of fruit in this cake gives it a delicious flavour.
The fruit provides sweetness, so there is no need for extra sugar.

NUTRITIONAL INFORMATION

Calories 423	Sugars 34g	
Protein 8g	Fat 16g	
Carbohydrate ...68g	Saturates 9g	

30 mins   1 hour

SERVES 8

INGREDIENTS

125 g/4¼ oz butter (chilled and cut into small pieces), plus extra for greasing

350 g/12 oz plain flour

2 tsp baking powder

1 tsp mixed spice powder

75 g/2¾ oz no-soak dried apricots, chopped

75 g/2¾ oz dried dates, chopped

75 g/2¾ oz glacé cherries, chopped

100 g/3½ oz raisins

125 ml/4 fl oz milk

2 eggs, beaten

grated rind of 1 orange

5–6 tbsp orange juice

3 tbsp clear honey

VARIATION

For a fruity alternative, replace the honey with 1 mashed ripe banana, if you prefer.

1 Grease a round 20 cm/8 inch cake tin with a little butter and line the base with baking parchment.

2 Sieve the flour, baking powder and mixed spice powder into a large mixing bowl.

3 Rub in the butter with your fingertips until the mixture resembles fine breadcrumbs.

4 Mix the apricots, dates, glacé cherries and raisins with the milk, beaten eggs, grated orange rind and orange juice.

5 Stir in the honey and add the fruit mixture to the dry ingredients, forming a soft, dropping consistency. Spoon into the prepared cake tin and level the surface.

6 Bake in a preheated oven, 180°C/350°F/Gas Mark 4, for 1 hour until a fine skewer inserted into the centre of the cake comes out clean.

7 Leave the cake to cool in the tin before turning out.

Apple Shortcakes

This American-style dessert is a sweet scone, split and filled with sliced apples and whipped cream. The shortcakes can be eaten warm or cold.

NUTRITIONAL INFORMATION

Calories 511   Sugars 44g
Protein . . . . .5g   Fat 24g
Carbohydrate . . .73g   Saturates 15g

 50 mins   15 mins

MAKES 4

INGREDIENTS

2 tbsp butter (chilled and cut into small pieces), plus extra for greasing

150 g/5½ oz plain flour

½ tsp salt

1 tsp baking powder

1 tbsp caster sugar

50 ml/2 fl oz milk

icing sugar, for dusting (optional)

FILLING

3 dessert apples, peeled, cored and sliced

100 g/3½ oz caster sugar

1 tbsp lemon juice

1 tsp ground cinnamon

300 ml/10 fl oz water

150 ml/5 fl oz double cream, lightly whipped

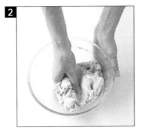

1 Lightly grease a baking tray. Sieve the flour, salt and baking powder into a mixing bowl. Stir in the sugar, then rub in the butter with your fingers until the mixture resembles fine breadcrumbs.

2 Add the milk and mix to a soft dough. On a floured surface, knead the dough and roll out to 1 cm/½ inch thick. Stamp out 4 rounds with a 5 cm/2 inch cutter. Transfer these to the prepared baking tray.

3 Bake in a preheated oven, 220°C/ 425°F/Gas Mark 7, for about 15 minutes until the shortcakes are well risen and lightly browned. Leave to cool.

4 To make the filling, place the apple, sugar, lemon juice, cinnamon and water in a pan. Bring to the boil and simmer, uncovered, for 5–10 minutes until the fruit is tender. Leave to cool a little. Remove the apples from the pan.

5 To serve, split the four shortcakes in half. Place each bottom half on an individual serving plate and spoon on a quarter of the apple slices, followed by the cream. Place the other half of the shortcake on top of the cream. Serve either warm or cold and dusted with icing sugar, if wished.

Treacle Scones

These scones are light and buttery like traditional scones, but they have a deliciously rich flavour which comes from the black treacle.

NUTRITIONAL INFORMATION

Calories 208	Sugars 9g	
Protein 4g	Fat 9g	
Carbohydrate ...30g	Saturates 6g	

35 mins   10 mins

SERVES 8

INGREDIENTS

6 tbsp butter (chilled and cut into small pieces), plus extra for greasing

225 g/8 oz self-raising flour

1 tbsp caster sugar

pinch of salt

1 dessert apple, peeled, cored and chopped

1 egg, beaten

2 tbsp black treacle

5 tbsp milk

1 Lightly grease a baking tray with a little butter.

2 Sieve the flour, sugar and salt into a mixing bowl.

3 Add the butter and rub it in with your fingertips until the mixture resembles fine breadcrumbs.

4 Stir the chopped apple into the mixture until thoroughly combined.

5 Mix the beaten egg, treacle and milk together in a jug. Add the mixture to the dry ingredients and mix well to form a soft dough.

6 On a lightly-floured working surface, roll out the dough to a thickness of 2 cm/¾ inch. Cut out 8 scones, using a 5 cm/2 inch cutter.

7 Arrange the Treacle Scones on the prepared baking tray and bake in a preheated oven, 220°C/425°F/Gas Mark 7, for 8–10 minutes.

8 Transfer the scones to a wire rack and leave to cool slightly before serving.

9 Serve split in half and spread with butter.

COOK'S TIP

These scones can be frozen, but are best defrosted and eaten within 1 month.

Cherry Scones

These are an alternative to traditional scones, using sweet glacé cherries which not only create colour but also add a distinct flavour.

NUTRITIONAL INFORMATION

Calories	211	Sugars	........10g
Protein	.........4g	Fat	..........9g
Carbohydrate	...31g	Saturates	......6g

 30 mins   10 mins

MAKES 8

INGREDIENTS

6 tbsp butter (chilled and cut into small pieces), plus extra for greasing

225 g/8 oz self-raising flour

15 g/½ oz caster sugar

pinch of salt

40 g/1½ oz glacé cherries, chopped

40 g/1½ oz sultanas

1 egg, beaten

50 ml/2 fl oz milk

1 Lightly grease a baking tray with a little butter.

2 Sieve the flour, sugar and salt into a mixing bowl and rub in the butter gently with your fingertips until the mixture resembles breadcrumbs.

3 Stir in the glacé cherries and sultanas. Add the egg.

4 Reserve 1 tablespoon of the milk for glazing, then add the remainder to the mixture. Mix well together to form a soft dough.

5 On a lightly-floured surface, roll out the dough to a thickness of 2 cm/¾ inch. Cut out 8 scones, using a 5 cm/2 inch cutter.

6 Place the scones on the prepared baking tray and brush the tops with the reserved milk.

7 Bake in a preheated oven, 220°C/425°F/Gas Mark 7, for 8–10 minutes or until the scones are golden brown.

8 Leave to cool on a wire rack, then serve split and buttered.

COOK'S TIP

These scones will freeze very successfully, but they are best defrosted and eaten within 1 month.

Rice Muffins with Amaretto

Italian rice gives these muffins an interesting texture. The amaretti biscuits complement the flavours and add a wonderful crunchy topping.

NUTRITIONAL INFORMATION

Calories 479   Sugars 24g
Protein ....7g   Fat 26g
Carbohydrate ...57g   Saturates 16g

25 mins   15 mins

MAKES 12

INGREDIENTS

2 tsp melted butter, for greasing

140 g/5 oz plain flour

1 tbsp baking powder

½ tsp bicarbonate of soda

½ tsp salt

1 egg

50 ml/2 fl oz honey

120 ml/4 fl oz milk

2 tbsp sunflower oil

½ tsp almond essence

60 g/2 oz cooked arborio rice

2–3 amaretti biscuits, coarsely crushed

AMARETTO BUTTER

115 g/4 oz unsalted butter
   (at room temperature)

1 tbsp honey

1–2 tbsp Amaretto liqueur

1–2 tbsp mascarpone cheese

1 Sieve the flour, baking powder, bicarbonate of soda and salt into a large bowl and stir together. Make a well in the centre.

2 In another bowl, beat the egg, honey, milk, oil and almond essence with an electric mixer for about 2 minutes until light and foamy. Gradually beat in the rice.

Pour this mixture into the prepared well and, using a fork, stir lightly until just combined. Do not over-beat; the mixture can be slightly lumpy.

3 Spoon the mixture into a lightly greased 12-cup muffin tin or into two 6-cup muffin tins. Sprinkle each muffin with some of the crushed amaretti biscuits and bake in a preheated oven, at 200°C/400°F/Gas Mark 6, for about 15 minutes until risen and golden; the tops should spring back lightly when pressed.

4 Cool in the tins on a wire rack for about 1 minute. Carefully remove the muffins and leave to cool slightly.

5 To make the Amaretto butter, place the butter and honey in a small bowl and beat until creamy. Add the Amaretto liqueur and mascarpone and beat together. Spoon into a small serving bowl and serve with the warm muffins.

COOK'S TIP
Use paper liners to line the muffin cups to prevent sticking.

Mini Orange Rice Cakes

These mini rice cakes, fragrant with orange (or sometimes lemon) rind, are found in many of the bakeries and coffee shops in Florence.

NUTRITIONAL INFORMATION

Calories 479	Sugars 24g	
Protein 7g	Fat 26g	
Carbohydrate ...57g	Saturates 16g	

 1 hour   20 mins

MAKES 16

INGREDIENTS

2 tsp melted butter, for greasing

700 ml/1¼ pints milk

pinch of salt

1 vanilla pod (split), seeds removed and reserved

100 g/3½ oz arborio rice

100 g/3½ oz sugar

25 g/1 oz butter

grated rind of 2 oranges

2 eggs, separated

2 tbsp orange-flavoured liqueur or rum

1 tbsp freshly squeezed orange juice

icing sugar, for dusting

1 orange (chopped), to decorate

1 Bring the milk to the boil in a large saucepan over a medium-high heat. Add the salt, vanilla pod and seeds, and sprinkle in the rice. Return to the boil, stirring once or twice. Reduce the heat and simmer, stirring frequently, for about 10 minutes.

2 Add the sugar and butter and continue to simmer for about 10 minutes, stirring frequently, until thick and creamy. Pour into a bowl and stir in the orange rind; remove the vanilla pod. Cool to room temperature, stirring the mixture occasionally.

3 In a separate bowl, beat the egg yolks with the liqueur and orange juice, then beat into the cooled rice mixture.

4 Beat the egg whites until they form soft peaks. Stir a spoonful into the rice mixture, then gently fold in the remaining whites.

5 Spoon the mixture into lightly greased muffin tins with 50 ml/2 fl oz cups, lined with paper liners. Fill to the brim. Bake in a preheated oven at 190°C/375°F/Gas Mark 5 for about 20 minutes until golden and cooked

through. Cool on a wire rack for 2 minutes, then remove the liners and cool completely. Decorate with chopped orange and dust with icing sugar before serving.

COOK'S TIP
Before boiling milk, rinse the saucepan with water to help prevent the milk from scorching.

Rich Chocolate Loaf

This chocolate dessert is made without baking, simply by combining its rich ingredients, and then chilling them.

NUTRITIONAL INFORMATION

Calories	180	Sugars	........16g
Protein	.........3g	Fat	...........11g
Carbohydrate	...18g	Saturates	.......5g

30 mins, plus refrigeration time

0 mins

MAKES 15 SLICES

INGREDIENTS

1 tsp melted butter, for greasing

75 g/2¾ oz almonds

150 g/5½ oz dark chocolate

75 g/2¾ oz butter, unsalted

210 ml/7½ fl oz canned condensed milk

2 tsp ground cinnamon

75 g/2¾ oz amaretti biscuits, broken

50 g/1¾ oz no-soak dried apricots, roughly chopped

1 Line a 650 g/1½ lb loaf tin with kitchen foil and grease very lightly.

2 Using a sharp knife, roughly chop the almonds.

3 Place the chocolate, butter, condensed milk and cinnamon in a heavy-based saucepan.

4 Heat the mixture over a low heat for 3–4 minutes, stirring constantly with a wooden spoon, until the chocolate has melted. Beat thoroughly.

5 Using a wooden spoon, stir the almonds, amaretti biscuits and apricots into the chocolate mixture, until completely incorporated.

6 Pour the mixture into the prepared tin and leave it to chill in the refrigerator for about 1 hour or until set.

7 Cut the Rich Chocolate Loaf into slices to serve.

COOK'S TIP

To melt chocolate, first break it into manageable pieces. The smaller the pieces, the quicker it will melt.

Fruit & Nut Loaf

This loaf is like a fruit-studded bread and may be served warm or cold, perhaps spread with a little margarine or butter, or topped with jam.

NUTRITIONAL INFORMATION

Calories	354	Sugars	........36g
Protein	.........8g	Fat	...........9g
Carbohydrate	...64g	Saturates	.....1.2g

  25 mins, plus rising time

 40 mins

SERVES 6

INGREDIENTS

225 g/8 oz white bread flour,
   plus extra for dusting

½ tsp salt

1 tbsp margarine, plus extra for greasing

2 tbsp light brown sugar

100 g/3½ oz sultanas

50 g/1¾ oz no-soak dried apricots, chopped

50 g/1¾ oz chopped hazelnuts

2 tsp easy-blend dried yeast

6 tbsp orange juice

6 tbsp natural yogurt

2 tbsp strained apricot jam

VARIATION

You can vary the nuts according to whatever you have at hand – try chopped walnuts or almonds.

1 Sift the flour and salt into a mixing bowl. Add the margarine and rub in with the fingertips. Stir in the sugar, sultanas, apricots, nuts and yeast.

2 Warm the orange juice in a saucepan, but do not allow to boil.

3 Stir the warm orange juice into the flour mixture, together with the natural yogurt, and bring the mixture together to form a dough.

4 Knead the dough on a lightly floured surface for 5 minutes, until smooth and elastic. Shape into a round and place on a lightly greased baking tray. Cover with a clean tea towel and leave to rise in a warm place until doubled in size.

5 Cook the loaf in a preheated oven, 220°C/425°F/Gas Mark 7, for 35–40 minutes, until cooked through. Transfer to a wire rack and brush with the apricot jam. Leave to cool before serving.

Fruity Muffins

These small cakes contain no butter, just a little corn oil. They are flavoured with banana, orange and apricot, so that every bite is deliciously tangy.

NUTRITIONAL INFORMATION

Calories	162	Sugars	11g
Protein	4g	Fat	4g
Carbohydrate	28g	Saturates	1g

 25 mins   30 mins

MAKES 10

INGREDIENTS

225 g/8 oz self-raising wholemeal flour

2 tsp baking powder

25 g/1 oz light muscovado sugar

100 g/3½ oz no-soak dried apricots, finely chopped

1 banana, mashed with 1 tbsp orange juice

1 tsp finely grated orange rind

300 ml/10 fl oz skimmed milk

1 egg, beaten

3 tbsp corn oil

2 tbsp porridge oats

fruit spread, honey, or maple syrup, to serve

1 Preheat the oven to 200°C/400°F/ Gas Mark 6. Place 10 paper muffin cases in a 12-cup muffin tin. Sift the flour and baking powder into a mixing bowl, adding any husks from the flour that remain in the sieve. Stir in the sugar and chopped apricots.

2 Make a well in the centre of the dry ingredients and add the banana, orange rind, milk, beaten egg and oil. Mix together well to form a thick batter. Divide the batter evenly among the muffin cases.

3 Sprinkle the uncooked muffins with some porridge oats and bake for 25–30 minutes until well risen and firm to the touch, or until a skewer inserted into the centre comes out clean. Transfer the muffins to a wire rack to cool a little. Serve them warm with a spoonful of fruit spread, honey or maple syrup.

VARIATION

If you like dried figs, they make a deliciously crunchy alternative to the apricots; they also go very well with the flavour of orange. Other no-soak dried fruits – chopped up finely – can be used as well.

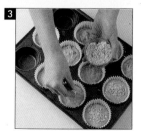

Chocolate Brownies

You really can have a low-fat chocolate treat. These moist bars contain a dried fruit purée that enables you to bake without adding any fat.

NUTRITIONAL INFORMATION

Calories 271	Sugars 45g
Protein 5g	Fat 4g
Carbohydrate . . .57g	Saturates 2g

40 mins · 30 mins

MAKES 12

I N G R E D I E N T S

2 tsp melted butter, for greasing

60 g/2¼ oz unsweetened stoned dates, chopped

60 g/2¼ oz no-soak dried prunes, chopped

6 tbsp unsweetened apple juice

4 eggs, beaten

300 g/10½ oz dark muscovado sugar

1 tsp vanilla essence

4 tbsp low-fat drinking chocolate powder, plus extra for dusting

2 tbsp cocoa powder

175 g/6 oz plain flour

60 g/2 oz dark chocolate chips

ICING

125 g/4¼ oz icing sugar

1–2 tsp water

1 tsp vanilla essence

1 Preheat the oven to 180°C/350°F/Gas Mark 4. Grease and line an 18 x 28 cm/7 x 11 inch cake tin with baking parchment. Place the dates and prunes in a small saucepan and add the apple juice. Bring to the boil, cover, and simmer for 10 minutes until soft. Beat to form a smooth purée, then set aside to cool.

2 Place the cooled fruit in a mixing bowl and stir in the eggs, sugar and vanilla essence. Sift in the drinking chocolate powder, cocoa and flour. Fold in, along with the chocolate chips, until thoroughly blended.

3 Spoon the mixture into the prepared tin and smooth over the top. Bake for 25–30 minutes until firm to the touch or until a skewer inserted into the centre comes out clean. Cut into 12 bars and leave to cool in the tin for 10 minutes. Transfer to a wire rack to cool completely.

4 To make the icing, sift the sugar into a bowl and mix with sufficient water and the vanilla essence to form a soft, but not too runny, icing.

5 Drizzle the icing over the chocolate brownies and allow to set. Dust with the extra chocolate powder before serving.

COOK'S TIP

Make double the amount, cut one of the cakes into bars and freeze, then store in a plastic bag in the freezer. Take out pieces of brownie as and when you need them – they will take no time at all to defrost.

Chocolate & Walnut Cake

This walnut-studded chocolate cake has a creamy butter icing.
It is perfect for entertaining because it can be made the day before.

NUTRITIONAL INFORMATION

Calories 555	Sugars 37g
Protein 6g	Fat 40g
Carbohydrate ...45g	Saturates 21g

45 mins   35 mins

SERVES 8

INGREDIENTS

2 tsp melted butter, for greasing

4 eggs

125 g/4¼ oz caster sugar

125 g/4¼ oz plain flour

1 tbsp cocoa powder

2 tbsp butter, melted

75 g/2¾ oz dark chocolate, melted

150 g/5½ oz walnuts, finely chopped

ICING

75 g/2¾ oz dark chocolate

125 g/4¼ oz butter

200 g/7 oz icing sugar

2 tbsp milk

walnut halves, to decorate

1 Grease a deep, round, 18 cm/7 inch cake tin and line the base. Place the eggs and caster sugar in a mixing bowl and whisk with an electric mixer for 10 minutes, or until light and foamy and the whisk leaves a trail that lasts a few seconds after the whisk is lifted.

2 Sieve the flour and cocoa powder together and fold into the eggs and sugar. Fold in the melted butter, chocolate and chopped walnuts. Pour into the tin and bake in a preheated oven, 160°C/325°F/Gas Mark 3, for 30–35 minutes, or until springy to the touch.

3 Leave to cool in the tin for 5 minutes, then transfer to a wire rack and leave to cool completely.

4 To make the icing, melt the dark chocolate and leave it to cool slightly. Beat together the butter, icing sugar and milk until the mixture is pale and fluffy. Whisk in the melted chocolate.

5 Cut the cake into 2 layers of equal thickness. Place the bottom half on a serving plate, spread with some of the icing, and put the other half on top. Smooth the remaining icing over the top of the cake with a spatula, swirling it slightly as you do so for a decorative effect. Decorate the cake with the walnut halves, and serve.

Banana & Cranberry Loaf

Chopped nuts, mixed peel, fresh orange juice and dried cranberries make this tea bread rich and moist.

NUTRITIONAL INFORMATION

Calories . . . . . . .388 Sugars 40g
Protein . . . . .5g Fat 17g
Carbohydrate . . .57g Saturates 2g

30 mins   1 hour

SERVES 8

I N G R E D I E N T S

2 tsp melted butter, for greasing

175 g/6 oz self-raising flour

½ tsp baking powder

150 g/5½ oz soft brown sugar

2 bananas, mashed

50 g/1¾ oz mixed peel, chopped

25 g/1 oz mixed nuts, chopped

50 g/1¾ oz dried cranberries

5–6 tbsp orange juice

2 eggs, beaten

150 ml/5 fl oz sunflower oil

75 g/2¾ oz icing sugar, sieved

grated rind of 1 orange

1 Grease a 900 g/2 lb loaf tin and line the base with baking parchment.

2 Sieve the flour and baking powder into a mixing bowl. Stir in the sugar, bananas, chopped mixed peel, nuts and dried cranberries.

3 Stir the orange juice, eggs and sunflower oil together until combined. Add the mixture to the dry ingredients and mix until well blended. Spoon the mixture into the prepared loaf tin and smooth the top.

4 Bake in a preheated oven, 180°C/ 350°F/Gas Mark 4, for about 1 hour, until firm to the touch or until a fine skewer inserted into the centre of the loaf comes out clean.

5 Turn out the loaf and leave it to cool on a wire rack.

6 Mix the icing sugar with a little water and drizzle the icing over the loaf. Sprinkle the orange rind over the top. Leave the icing to set before serving the loaf in slices.

COOK'S TIP
This tea bread will keep for a couple of days. Wrap it carefully and store in a cool, dry place.

Chocolate & Apricot Squares

The inclusion of white chocolate makes this a very rich cake, so serve it cut into small squares or bars, or sliced thinly.

NUTRITIONAL INFORMATION

Calories ....295 Sugars 23g
Protein ....6g Fat 15g
Carbohydrate ...36g Saturates 9g

 30 mins   30 mins

SERVES 12

INGREDIENTS

125 g/4¼ oz butter, plus extra for greasing

175 g/6 oz white chocolate, chopped

4 eggs

125 g/4¼ oz caster sugar

200 g/7 oz plain flour, sieved

1 tsp baking powder

pinch of salt

100 g/3½ oz no-soak dried apricots, chopped

1 Lightly grease a square 20 cm/9 inch cake tin and line the base with a sheet of baking parchment.

2 Melt the butter and chocolate in a heatproof bowl set over a saucepan of simmering water. Stir the mixture frequently with a wooden spoon until it is smooth and glossy. Leave to cool slightly.

3 Beat the eggs and caster sugar into the butter and chocolate mixture until well combined.

4 Fold in the flour, baking powder, salt and chopped dried apricots. Mix together well.

5 Pour the mixture into the cake tin and bake in an oven preheated to 180°C/ 350°F/Gas Mark 4, for between 25–30 minutes.

6 The centre of the cake may not be completely firm, but it will set as it cools. Leave it in the tin to cool.

7 When the cake is completely cold, turn it out and slice it into small squares or bars.

VARIATION

Replace the white chocolate with milk or dark chocolate, if you prefer.

Carrot Cake

This classic favourite is always popular with children and adults when it appears on the table at a children;s tea party.

NUTRITIONAL INFORMATION

Calories	294	Sugars	.......32g
Protein	.........3g	Fat	..........15g
Carbohydrate	...40g	Saturates	.......5g

30 mins   25 mins

12 BARS

INGREDIENTS

2 tsp melted butter, for greasing

125 g/4¼ oz self-raising flour

pinch of salt

1 tsp ground cinnamon

125 g/4¼ oz soft brown sugar

2 eggs

100 ml/3½ fl oz sunflower oil

125 g/4½ oz carrots, peeled and finely grated

25 g/1 oz desiccated coconut

25 g/1 oz walnuts, chopped

walnut pieces, for decoration

ICING

4 tbsp butter, softened

50 g/1¾ oz full-fat soft cheese

225 g/8 oz icing sugar, sieved

1 tsp lemon juice

1 Lightly grease a square 20 cm/8 inch cake tin. Line with baking parchment.

2 Sieve the flour, salt and ground cinnamon into a large bowl and stir in the brown sugar. Add the eggs and oil to the dry ingredients and mix well.

3 Stir in the grated carrot, desiccated coconut and chopped walnuts.

4 Pour the mixture into the prepared tin and bake in a preheated oven, 180°C/350°F/Gas Mark 4, for 20–25 minutes or until just firm to the touch. Leave to cool in the tin.

5 Meanwhile, make the cheese icing. In a bowl, beat together the butter, full-fat soft cheese, icing sugar and lemon juice until the mixture has a fluffy and creamy texture.

6 Turn the cake out of the tin and cut into 12 bars or slices. Spread with the icing and decorate with walnut pieces.

VARIATION

For a more moist cake, replace the coconut with 1 roughly mashed banana.

Coconut Cake

This is a great family favourite, perfect for including in a lunch-box or a picnic hamper, and for serving as an afternoon treat.

NUTRITIONAL INFORMATION

Calories 464	Sugars 20g	
Protein 8g	Fat 26g	
Carbohydrate . . .54g	Saturates 18g	

 25 mins   1 hour

MAKES 6-8

I N G R E D I E N T S

100 g/3½ oz butter (cut into small pieces), plus extra for greasing

225 g/8 oz self-raising flour

¼ tsp salt

100 g/3½ oz demerara sugar

100 g/3½ oz desiccated coconut, plus extra for sprinkling

2 eggs, beaten

4 tbsp milk

COOK'S TIP
The flavour of this cake is enhanced by storing it in a cool, dry place for a few days before eating.

1 Grease a 900 g/2 lb loaf tin and line the base with baking parchment.

2 Sieve the flour and a pinch of salt into a mixing bowl and rub in the butter with your fingertips until the mixture resembles fine breadcrumbs.

3 Stir in the demerara sugar, coconut, eggs and milk and mix to a soft, dropping consistency.

4 Spoon the mixture into the prepared tin and level the surface. Bake in a preheated oven, 160°C/325°F/Gas Mark 3, for 30 minutes.

5 Remove the cake from the oven and sprinkle with the extra coconut. Return the cake to the oven and cook for a further 30 minutes until well risen and golden, or a fine skewer inserted into the centre comes out clean.

6 Leave the cake to cool in the tin before turning it out and transferring it to a wire rack where it can be left to cool completely before serving.

Spiced Apple Ring

Adding fresh apple pieces and flaked almonds to the cake mixture makes this ring-shaped cake beautifully moist, yet crunchy.

NUTRITIONAL INFORMATION

Calories ....479 Sugars 24g
Protein ....7g Fat 26g
Carbohydrate ...57g Saturates 16g

 25 mins   30 mins

SERVES 8

I N G R E D I E N T S

175 g/6 oz butter, softened

175 g/6 oz caster sugar

3 eggs, beaten

175 g/6 oz self-raising flour

1 tsp ground cinnamon

1 tsp ground mixed spice

2 dessert apples, cored and grated

2 tbsp apple juice or milk

25 g/1 oz flaked almonds

1 Lightly grease a 25 cm/10 inch ovenproof ring mould.

2 In a mixing bowl, cream together the butter and sugar until light and fluffy. Gradually add the beaten eggs, beating well after each addition.

3 Sieve the flour and the spices, then carefully fold them into the creamed mixture.

4 Stir in the grated apples and the apple juice or milk. Mix to a soft, dropping consistency.

5 Sprinkle the flaked almonds around the base of the mould and spoon the cake mixture on top. Level the surface.

6 Bake the ring in a preheated oven, at 180°C/350°F/Gas Mark 4, for about 30 minutes until well risen, or until a fine skewer inserted into the centre comes out clean.

7 Leave the cake to cool in the tin before turning out and transferring to a wire rack to cool completely. Serve the Spiced Apple Ring cut into slices.

COOK'S TIP

This cake can also be made in a round 18 cm/7 inch cake tin if you do not have an ovenproof ring mould.

Gingerbread

This wonderfully spicy gingerbread has a deliciously moist texture, created by the addition of chopped fresh apples.

NUTRITIONAL INFORMATION

Calories 248   Sugars 21g
Protein . . . . .3g   Fat 11g
Carbohydrate . . .36g   Saturates 7g

 30 mins   35 mins

12 BARS

INGREDIENTS

150 g/5½ oz butter, plus extra for greasing

175 g/6 oz soft light brown sugar

2 tbsp black treacle

225 g/8 oz plain flour

1 tsp baking powder

2 tsp bicarbonate of soda

2 tsp ground ginger

150 ml/5 fl oz milk

1 egg, beaten

2 dessert apples, peeled, chopped and coated with 1 tbsp lemon juice

1 Grease a square 23 cm/9 inch cake tin and line with baking parchment.

2 Melt the butter, sugar and treacle in a saucepan over a low heat and set the mixture aside to cool.

3 Sieve the flour, baking powder, bicarbonate of soda and ginger into a mixing bowl.

4 Stir in the milk, beaten egg and buttery liquid, followed by the chopped apples coated with the lemon juice.

5 Mix everything together gently, then pour the mixture into the prepared tin and smooth the surface.

6 Bake in a preheated oven, 160°C/325°F/Gas Mark 3, for 30–35 minutes, until the cake has risen and a fine skewer inserted into the centre comes out clean.

7 Leave the cake to cool completely in the tin. Then carefully turn it out on to a board or plate before cutting into 12 bars for serving.

VARIATION

If you enjoy the flavour of ginger, try adding 25 g/1 oz finely chopped stem ginger to the mixture in step 3.

Cranberry Muffins

These savoury muffins are an ideal accompaniment to soup, and they make a nice change from sweet cakes for serving with coffee.

NUTRITIONAL INFORMATION

Calories	96	Sugars	4g
Protein	3g	Fat	4g
Carbohydrate	14g	Saturates	2g

🍐 🍐 🍐

25 mins   20 mins

SERVES 18

INGREDIENTS

2 tsp melted butter, for greasing

225 g/8 oz plain flour

2 tsp baking powder

½ tsp salt

50 g/1¾ oz caster sugar

4 tbsp butter, melted

2 eggs, beaten

200 ml/7 fl oz milk

100 g/3½ oz fresh cranberries

35 g/1¼ oz Parmesan cheese, freshly grated

1 Lightly grease 18 cups in 2 12-cup muffin tins. Sieve the flour, baking powder and salt into a mixing bowl. Stir in the caster sugar.

2 In a separate bowl, mix the butter, beaten eggs and milk together, then pour into the bowl of dry ingredients. Mix lightly together until all of the ingredients are evenly combined. Finally, stir in the fresh cranberries.

3 Divide the mixture between the prepared muffin tins. Sprinkle the grated Parmesan cheese over the top of each muffin.

4 Bake in a preheated oven, 200°C/400°F/Gas Mark 6, for about 20 minutes, or until the muffins are well risen and a golden brown colour.

5 Leave the Cranberry Muffins to cool in the tins, then carefully transfer them on to a wire rack and leave to cool completely before serving.

VARIATION

For a sweet alternative to this recipe, replace the Parmesan cheese with demerara sugar in step 4, if you prefer.

Cinnamon & Seed Squares

These moist squares have a lovely spicy flavour. They smell simply wonderful while they are cooking.

NUTRITIONAL INFORMATION

Calories ....397 Sugars 23g
Protein ....6g Fat 25g
Carbohydrate ...40g Saturates 14g

  30 mins   45 mins

MAKES 12

INGREDIENTS

250 g/9 oz butter (softened), plus extra for greasing

250 g/9 oz caster sugar

3 eggs, beaten

250 g/9 oz self-raising flour

½ tsp bicarbonate of soda

1 tbsp ground cinnamon

150 ml/5 fl oz soured cream

100 g/3½ oz sunflower seeds

1 Grease a square 23 cm/9 inch cake tin with butter and line the base with baking parchment.

2 In a large mixing bowl, cream together the butter and caster sugar until the mixture is light and fluffy.

3 Gradually add the beaten eggs to the mixture, beating thoroughly after each addition.

4 Sieve the self-raising flour, bicarbonate of soda and ground cinnamon into the creamed mixture and fold in gently, using a metal spoon.

5 Spoon in the soured cream and sunflower seeds and gently mix until well combined.

6 Spoon the mixture into the prepared cake tin and level the surface with the back of a spoon or a knife.

7 Bake in a preheated oven, 180°C/ 350°F/Gas Mark 4, for about 45 minutes until the mixture is firm to the touch when pressed with a finger.

8 Loosen the edges with a round-bladed knife, then turn out on to a wire rack to cool. Slice into 12 squares.

COOK'S TIP

These moist squares freeze well and will keep for up to 1 month.

Hazelnut Squares

Quick and easy to make for an afternoon treat. The chopped hazelnuts can be replaced by any other nut of your choice.

NUTRITIONAL INFORMATION

Calories 163	Sugars 10g	
Protein 2g	Fat 10g	
Carbohydrate ...18g	Saturates 4g	

25 mins   25 mins

MAKES 16

INGREDIENTS

100 g/3½ oz butter (chilled and cut into small pieces), plus extra for greasing

150 g/5½ oz plain flour

¼ tsp salt

1 tsp baking powder

150 g/5½ oz soft light brown sugar

1 egg, beaten

4 tbsp milk

100 g/3½ oz hazelnuts, halved

demerara sugar, for sprinkling (optional)

1 Grease a square 23 cm/9 inch cake tin with butter and line the base with baking parchment.

2 Sieve the flour, together with a pinch of salt and the baking powder, into a large mixing bowl.

3 Add the butter and rub it in with your fingertips until the mixture resembles fine breadcrumbs. Add the soft brown sugar and stir to mix.

4 Add the beaten egg, milk and halved hazelnuts to the dry ingredients and stir well until thoroughly combined and a soft consistency.

5 Spoon the mixture into the prepared cake tin and level the surface. Sprinkle with demerara sugar, if using.

6 Bake in a preheated oven, 180°C/ 350°F/Gas Mark 4, for about 25 minutes or until the mixture is firm to the touch when pressed.

7 Leave to cool for 10 minutes, then loosen the edges with a round-bladed knife and turn out on to a wire rack. Cut into squares.

VARIATION
For a coffee-time biscuit, replace the milk with the same amount of cold, strong black coffee – the stronger the better!

Rock Drops

These rock drops are more substantial than a crisp biscuit.
Serve them fresh from the oven to enjoy them at their best.

NUTRITIONAL INFORMATION

Calories	270	Sugars	. . . . . . .21g
Protein	. . . . .4g	Fat	. . . . .11g
Carbohydrate	. . .41g	Saturates	. . . . . . .7g

 25 mins   20 mins

MAKES 8

I N G R E D I E N T S

100 g/3½ oz butter (cut into small pieces),
    plus extra for greasing

200 g/7 oz plain flour

2 tsp baking powder

75 g/2¾ oz demerara sugar

100 g/3½ oz sultanas

25 g/1 oz glacé cherries, finely chopped

1 egg, beaten

2 tbsp milk

1 Lightly grease a baking tray with a little butter. Preheat the oven to 200°C/400°F/Gas Mark 6.

2 Sieve the flour and baking powder into a mixing bowl. Rub in the butter with your fingertips until the mixture resembles breadcrumbs.

3 Stir in the sugar, sultanas and chopped glacé cherries and mix thoroughly.

4 Add the beaten egg and the milk to the mixture and mix to form a soft dough.

5 Spoon 8 mounds of the mixture on to the prepared baking tray, spacing them well apart as they will spread while they are cooking.

6 Bake for 15–20 minutes, until firm to the touch when pressed with a finger.

7 Remove the rock drops from the baking tray. Either serve piping hot from the oven or transfer to a wire rack and leave to cool before serving.

COOK'S TIP

For convenience, prepare the dry ingredients in advance and stir in the liquid just before cooking.

Chocolate Chip Brownies

Choose a good-quality chocolate for these chocolate chip brownies to give them a rich flavour that is not too sweet.

NUTRITIONAL INFORMATION

Calories	388	Sugars	.......40g
Protein	.........5g	Fat	..........17g
Carbohydrate	...57g	Saturates	.......2g

25 mins   35 mins

MAKES 12

I N G R E D I E N T S

150 g/5½ oz dark chocolate, broken into pieces

225 g/8 oz butter, softened

225 g/8 oz self-raising flour

125 g/4¼ oz caster sugar

4 eggs, beaten

75 g/2¾ oz pistachio nuts, chopped

100 g/3½ oz white chocolate, roughly chopped

icing sugar, for dusting

1 Lightly grease a 23 cm/9 inch baking tin and line with baking parchment.

2 Melt the dark chocolate and butter in a heatproof bowl set over a saucepan of simmering water. Leave to cool slightly.

3 Sieve the flour into a separate mixing bowl and stir in the caster sugar.

4 Stir the eggs into the melted chocolate mixture, then pour into the flour and sugar mixture, beating well. Stir in the pistachio nuts and white chocolate. Pour the brownie mixture into the tin, using a palette knife to spread it evenly into the corners.

  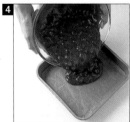

5 Bake in a preheated oven, 180°C/ 350°F/Gas Mark 4, for 30–35 minutes until firm to the touch. Leave to cool in the tin for 20 minutes, then turn the block of cake out on to a wire rack.

6 Dust with icing sugar and cut into 12 pieces when cold.

COOK'S TIP
The brownie will not be completely firm in the middle when it is removed from the oven, but it will set when it has cooled.

Torta del Cielo

This almond-flavoured sponge cake has a dense, moist texture which melts in the mouth. The perfect accompaniment to a cup of coffee.

NUTRITIONAL INFORMATION

Calories	795	Sugars	........46g
Protein	........14g	Fat	.........51g
Carbohydrate	...76g	Saturates	......23g

 25 mins 50 mins

SERVES 4-6

I N G R E D I E N T S

225 g/8 oz unsalted butter (at room temperature), plus extra for greasing

175g/6 oz raw almonds (in their skins)

200 g/7 oz sugar, plus 2 tbsp

3 eggs, lightly beaten

1 tsp almond essence

1 tsp vanilla essence

75 g/2¾oz plain flour

pinch of salt

TO SERVE

icing sugar, for dusting

flaked almonds, toasted

1 Lightly grease a round or square 20 cm/8 inch cake tin and line with baking parchment.

2 Place the almonds in a food processor and grind until a crumbly mixture.

3 In a bowl, beat together the butter and sugar until smooth and fluffy. Beat in the almonds, eggs, and almond and vanilla essences. Blend well.

4 Stir in the flour and salt and mix together briefly, until the flour is just incorporated.

5 Pour or spoon the mixture into the greased tin and smooth the surface. Bake in a preheated oven at 180°C/350°F/Gas Mark 4 for 40–50 minutes, or until the cake feels spongy when pressed.

6 Remove the tin from the oven, and leave on a wire rack to cool completely. To serve, dust the cake with icing sugar and decorate with the toasted flaked almonds.

Panforte di Siena

This famous Tuscan honey and nut cake is a Christmas speciality.
In Italy it is sold in pretty boxes, and served in very thin slices.

NUTRITIONAL INFORMATION

Calories . . . . . . .257 Sugars 29g
Protein . . . . .5g Fat 13g
Carbohydrate . . .33g Saturates 1g

45 mins   1 hour

SERVES 12

I N G R E D I E N T S

125 g/4¼ oz whole almonds, split

125 g/4¼ oz hazelnuts

90 g/3¼ oz mixed peel, chopped

60 g/2¼ oz no-soak dried apricots

60 g/2¼ oz glacé pineapple

grated rind of 1 large orange

60 g/2¼ oz plain flour

2 tbsp cocoa powder

2 tsp ground cinnamon

125 g/4¼ oz caster sugar

175 g/6 oz honey

icing sugar, for decoration

1 Toast the almonds under the grill until lightly browned, and then place in a bowl.

2 Toast the hazelnuts until the skins split. Place on a dry tea towel and rub off the skins. Roughly chop the hazelnuts and add them to the almonds, together with the mixed peel.

3 Chop the apricots and pineapple fairly finely and add to the nuts, together with the orange rind. Mix well.

4 Sieve the flour, cocoa and cinnamon into the nut mixture and mix well.

5 Line a round 20 cm/8 inch cake tin or deep, loose-based flan tin with baking parchment.

6 Put the sugar and honey into a saucepan and heat until the sugar dissolves. Boil gently for about 5 minutes, or until the mixture thickens and begins to turn a deeper shade of brown. Quickly add to the nut mixture and mix thoroughly.

Turn into the prepared tin and level the top using the back of a damp spoon.

7 Cook in a preheated oven, at 150°C/300°F/Gas Mark 2, for 1 hour. Remove from the oven and leave in the tin until completely cool. Take out of the tin and carefully peel off the paper. Before serving, decorate the cake by dredging with sifted icing sugar. Serve in thin slices.

White Truffle Cake

A light white sponge, topped with a rich creamy-white chocolate truffle mixture, makes an out-of-this-world gateau.

NUTRITIONAL INFORMATION

Calories 358	Sugars 26g	
Protein 6g	Fat 25g	
Carbohydrate ...29g	Saturates 15g	

40 mins, plus refrigeration time   25 mins

SERVES 12

I N G R E D I E N T S

2 eggs

50 g/1¾ oz caster sugar

50 g/1¾ oz plain flour

50 g/1¾ oz white chocolate, melted

T R U F F L E   T O P P I N G

300 ml/10 fl oz double cream

350 g/12 oz white chocolate, broken into pieces

250 g/9 oz Quark or fromage frais

T O   D E C O R A T E

350 g/12 oz dark, milk or white chocolate caraque

cocoa powder, to dust

1 Grease a round 20 cm/8 inch springform tin and line the base.

2 Whisk the eggs and caster sugar in a mixing bowl for 10 minutes, or until very light and foamy and the whisk leaves a trail that lasts a few seconds when the whisk is lifted out. Sieve the flour and fold in with a metal spoon. Fold in the melted white chocolate. Pour into the tin and bake in a preheated oven, 180°C/ 350°F/Gas Mark 4, for 25 minutes or until springy to the touch. Leave to cool slightly, then transfer to a wire rack until completely cold. Return the cold cake to the tin.

3 To make the topping, place the cream in a pan and bring to the boil, stirring constantly. Cool slightly, then add the white chocolate and stir until melted and combined. Remove from the heat and leave until almost cool, stirring, then mix in the fromage frais. Pour on top of the cake and chill for 2 hours.

4 To make the chocolate caraque, pour melted chocolate on to a marble or acrylic board and spread thinly with a spatula. Leave to set. Using a scraper, push through the chocolate at a 25° angle until a large curl forms. Chill each curl until set, and then use to decorate the cake. Sprinkle with cocoa powder.

Rich Fruit Cake

Prepare this moist, fruit-laden cake for a special occasion.
It would also make an excellent Christmas cake.

NUTRITIONAL INFORMATION

Calories ....772 Sugars 137g
Protein ....14g Fat 5g
Carbohydrate ..179g Saturates 1g

40 mins   1½ hours

SERVES 4

INGREDIENTS

175 g/6 oz unsweetened pitted dates

125 g/4¼ oz no-soak dried prunes

200 ml/7 fl oz unsweetened orange juice

2 tbsp treacle

1 tsp finely grated lemon rind

1 tsp finely grated orange rind

225 g/8 oz self-raising wholemeal flour

1 tsp mixed spice

125 g/4¼ oz seedless raisins

125 g/4¼ oz sultanas

125 g/4¼ oz currants

125 g/4¼ oz dried cranberries

3 large eggs, separated

TO DECORATE

1 tbsp apricot jam, softened

icing sugar, to dust

175 g/6 oz ready-made royal icing

strips of orange rind

strips of lemon rind

1 Preheat the oven to 160°C/325°F/Gas Mark 3. Grease and line a deep, round 20 cm/8 inch cake tin. Chop the dates and prunes and place in a pan with the orange juice. Simmer for 10 minutes. Remove from the heat and beat the fruit mixture until puréed. Add the treacle, orange and lemon rinds. Allow to cool.

2 Sieve the flour and spice into a bowl, adding any husks that remain in the sieve. Add the dried fruit. When the date and prune mixture is cool, whisk in the egg yolks. In a clean bowl, whisk the egg whites until stiff. Spoon the fruit mixture into the dry ingredients and mix together.

3 Gently fold in the egg whites using a metal spoon. Transfer the mixture to the prepared tin and bake for 1½ hours. Leave to cool.

4 Remove the cake from the tin and brush the top with apricot jam. Dust the work surface with icing sugar and roll out the royal icing thinly. Lay it over the top of the cake and trim the edges. Decorate the cake with the strips of orange and lemon rind.

Chocolate Brownie Roulade

This delicious dessert is inspired by chocolate brownies. The addition of nuts and raisins gives it extra texture.

NUTRITIONAL INFORMATION

Calories 436	Sugars 38g	
Protein 7g	Fat 30g	
Carbohydrate ...38g	Saturates 16g	

45 mins   25 mins

SERVES 8

I N G R E D I E N T S

2 tsp melted butter, for greasing

150 g/5 ½ oz dark chocolate, broken into pieces

3 tbsp water

175 g/6 oz caster sugar

5 eggs, separated

25 g/1 oz raisins, chopped

25 g/1 oz pecan nuts, chopped

pinch of salt

icing sugar, for dusting

300 ml/10 fl oz double cream, whipped lightly

1 Grease a 30 x 20 cm/12 x 8 inch Swiss roll tin, line with baking parchment and grease the parchment.

2 Place the chocolate, with the water, in a small saucepan over a low heat, stirring until the chocolate has just melted. Leave to cool a little.

3 In a bowl, whisk the sugar and egg yolks for 2–3 minutes with an electric whisk until thick and pale. Fold in the cooled chocolate, raisins and pecan nuts.

4 In a separate bowl, whisk the egg whites with the salt. Fold one quarter of the egg whites into the chocolate mixture, then fold in the rest of the whites, working lightly and quickly.

5 Transfer the mixture to the prepared tin and bake in a preheated oven, 180°C/350°F/Gas Mark 4, for 25 minutes, until risen and just firm to the touch. Leave to cool before covering with a sheet of non-stick baking parchment and a damp, clean tea towel. Leave to stand until completely cold.

6 Turn the roulade on to another piece of baking parchment dusted with icing sugar. Remove the lining parchment.

7 Spread the whipped cream over the roulade. Starting from a short end, roll the sponge away from you, using the paper to guide you. Trim the ends of the roulade to make a neat finish and transfer to a serving plate. Leave the roulade to chill in the refrigerator until ready to serve. Dust with a little more icing sugar.

Chocolate Slab Cake

This chocolate slab cake gets its moist texture from the soured cream that is stirred into the beaten mixture.

NUTRITIONAL INFORMATION

Calories	423	Sugars	.......40g
Protein	.........3g	Fat	.........28g
Carbohydrate	...43g	Saturates	......17g

25 mins   45 mins

SERVES 10

INGREDIENTS

225 g/8 oz butter, plus extra for greasing

100 g/3½ oz dark chocolate, chopped

150 ml/5 fl oz water

300 g/10½ oz plain flour

2 tsp baking powder

275 g/9½ oz soft brown sugar

150 ml/5 fl oz soured cream

2 eggs, beaten

ICING

200 g/7 oz dark chocolate

6 tbsp water

3 tbsp single cream

15 g/½ oz butter, chilled

1 Grease a square 33 x 20 cm/13 x 8 inch cake tin and line the base with baking parchment. In a saucepan, melt the butter and chocolate with the water over a low heat, stirring frequently.

2 Sieve the flour and baking powder into a mixing bowl and stir in the sugar. Add the hot chocolate liquid and beat well. Stir in the cream and eggs.

3 Pour the cake mixture into the prepared tin and bake in a preheated oven, 190°C/375°F/Gas Mark 5, for 40–45 minutes.

4 Leave the cake to cool in the tin before turning it out on to a wire rack. Leave it to cool completely.

5 To make the icing, melt the chocolate with the water in a saucepan over a very low heat. Stir in the cream, then remove from the heat and add the butter. Pour the icing over the cake, using a spatula to spread it evenly.

COOK'S TIP

Leave the cake on the wire rack to ice it and place a large baking tray underneath to catch any drips.

Chocolate & Almond Torte

This torte is perfect for serving on a hot, sunny day with double cream and a selection of fresh summer berries.

NUTRITIONAL INFORMATION

Calories	....	.399	Sugars	....	.30g
Protein	....	5g	Fat	....	.28g
Carbohydrate	...36g	Saturates	......	14g

 35 mins   45 mins

SERVES 10

INGREDIENTS

2 tsp melted butter, for greasing

225 g/8 oz dark chocolate, broken into pieces

3 tbsp water

150 g/5½ oz soft brown sugar

175 g/6 oz butter, softened

25 g/1 oz ground almonds

3 tbsp self-raising flour

5 eggs, separated

100 g/3½ oz almonds, blanched and finely chopped

icing sugar, for dusting

double cream, to serve (optional)

COOK'S TIP

For a nuttier flavour, toast the chopped almonds in a dry frying pan over a medium heat for about 2 minutes, until lightly golden.

1 Grease a 23 cm/9 inch loose-bottomed cake tin and line the base with baking parchment.

2 In a saucepan set over a very low heat, melt the chocolate with the water, stirring until smooth. Add the sugar and stir until dissolved, taking the pan off the heat to prevent it overheating.

3 Add the butter, in small amounts, until it has melted into the chocolate. Remove from the heat and lightly stir in the ground almonds and flour. Add the egg yolks one at a time, beating well after each addition.

4 In a large mixing bowl, whisk the egg whites until they stand in soft peaks,

then fold them into the chocolate mixture with a metal spoon. Stir in the chopped almonds. Pour the mixture into the tin and level the surface.

5 Bake in a preheated oven, at 180°C/ 350°F/Gas Mark 4, for about 40–45 minutes until well risen and firm. It is normal for the cake to crack on the surface during cooking.

6 Leave to cool in the tin for 30–40 minutes. Turn out on to a wire rack to cool completely. Dust with icing sugar and serve in slices with double cream, if using.

Orange Kugelhopf Cake

This moist cake is full of the flavour of fresh oranges, and baking it in a deep, fluted kugelhopf tin ensures that you create a stunning shape.

NUTRITIONAL INFORMATION

Calories 877	Sugars 82g
Protein 12g	Fat 35g
Carbohydrate . .137g	Saturates 21g

  1 hour   55 mins

SERVES 4

INGREDIENTS

225 g/8 oz butter (softened) plus extra for greasing

225 g/8 oz caster sugar

4 eggs, separated

425 g/15 oz plain flour, plus extra for dusting

pinch of salt

3 tsp baking powder

300 ml/10 fl oz fresh orange juice

1 tbsp orange flower water

1 tsp grated orange rind

SYRUP

200 ml/7 fl oz orange juice

200 g/7 oz granulated sugar

1 Grease and flour a 25 cm/10 inch kugelhopf tin or deep ring mould.

2 In a bowl, cream together the butter and caster sugar until the mixture is light and fluffy. Add the egg yolks, one at a time, whisking the mixture thoroughly after each addition.

3 Sieve together the flour, a pinch of salt and the baking powder in a separate bowl. Gently fold the dry ingredients and the orange juice alternately into the creamed mixture with

a metal spoon, working as lightly as possible. Stir in the orange flower water and orange rind.

4 Briskly whisk the egg whites until they form soft peaks and then fold them into the mixture in a figure-of-eight movement.

5 Pour the mixture into the prepared tin or ring mould and bake in a preheated oven, 180°C/350°F/Gas Mark 4, for about 50–55 minutes, or until a metal skewer inserted into the centre of the cake comes out clean.

6 For the syrup, bring the orange juice and sugar to the boil in a saucepan over a low heat, then simmer for 5 minutes until the sugar has dissolved.

7 Remove the cake from the oven and leave to one side to cool in the tin for 10 minutes. Prick the cake all over with a fine skewer and brush with half of the syrup. Leave the cake to cool for a further 10 minutes. Invert the cake on to a wire rack placed over a deep plate. Brush the syrup generously over the cake until it is entirely covered. Serve the cake warm or cold.

Marbled Chocolate Cake

Separate chocolate and orange cake mixtures are combined in a ring mould to achieve the marbled effect in this light sponge.

NUTRITIONAL INFORMATION

Calories	388	Sugars	.......40g
Protein	.........5g	Fat	..........17g
Carbohydrate	...57g	Saturates	.......2g

 40 mins   35 mins

SERVES 8

INGREDIENTS

175 g/6 oz butter (softened), plus extra for greasing

175 g/6 oz caster sugar

3 eggs, beaten

150 g/5½ oz self-raising flour, sieved

25 g/1 oz cocoa powder, sifted

5–6 tbsp orange juice

grated rind of 1 orange

1 Lightly grease a 25 cm/10 inch ovenproof ring mould.

2 In a mixing bowl, cream together the butter and sugar with an electric whisk for about 5 minutes.

3 Add the beaten egg a little at a time, whisking well after each addition.

4 Using a metal spoon, fold the flour into the creamed mixture carefully, then spoon half of the mixture into a separate mixing bowl.

5 Fold the cocoa powder and half of the orange juice into the mixture in one of the bowls and mix gently.

6 Fold the remaining orange juice and orange rind into the mixture in the other bowl and mix gently.

7 Place spoonfuls of each of the mixtures alternately into the mould, then drag a skewer through the mixture to create a marbled effect.

8 Bake in a preheated oven, 180°C/350°F/Gas Mark 4, for 30–35 minutes until well risen, and a skewer inserted into the cake comes out clean.

9 Leave the cake to cool in the mould before turning out on to a wire rack.

VARIATION

For a richer chocolate flavour, add 40 g/1½ oz chocolate drops to the cocoa mixture.

Coffee Streusel Cake

This cake has a moist coffee and almond sponge on the bottom, covered with a crisp, crunchy, spicy topping.

NUTRITIONAL INFORMATION

Calories	409	Sugars	........21g
Protein	.........8g	Fat	..........19g
Carbohydrate	...55g	Saturates	.....10g

35 mins   1 hour

SERVES 8

INGREDIENTS

2 tsp melted butter, for greasing

275 g/9½ oz plain flour

1 tbsp baking powder

75 g/2¾ oz caster sugar

150 ml/5 fl oz milk

2 eggs

100 g/3½ oz butter, melted and cooled

2 tbsp instant coffee mixed with 1 tbsp boiling water

50 g/1¾ oz almonds, chopped

TOPPING

75 g/2¾ oz self-raising flour

75 g/2¾ oz demerara sugar

2 tbsp butter, cut into small pieces

1 tsp ground mixed spice

1 tbsp water

icing sugar, for dusting

1 Grease a round 23 cm/9 inch loose-bottomed cake tin with butter and line with baking parchment. Sieve the flour and baking powder into a large mixing bowl, then stir in the caster sugar.

2 Whisk the milk, eggs, butter and coffee mixture and pour on to the dry ingredients. Add the almonds and mix lightly together. Spoon into the tin.

3 To make the topping, mix the flour and demerara sugar together in a separate bowl.

4 Add the butter and rub it in with your fingertips until a crumbly mixture is formed. Sprinkle in the ground mixed spice, pour in the water and bring the mixture together until it resembles loose crumbs. Sprinkle the topping evenly over the surface of the cake mixture in the tin.

5 Bake in a preheated oven, 190°C/375°F/Gas Mark 5, for about 1 hour. Cover the cake loosely with kitchen foil if the topping starts to brown too quickly. Leave to cool in the tin, then turn out. Dust with icing sugar just before serving.

Risotto Cake with Berries

Served with your favourite summer berries and scented mascarpone cream, this baked sweet risotto makes an unusual dessert.

NUTRITIONAL INFORMATION

Calories 319   Sugars 30g
Protein . . . . .8g   Fat 9g
Carbohydrate . . .54g   Saturates 4g

45 mins, plus refrigeration time   20 mins

SERVES 6-8

INGREDIENTS

2 tsp melted butter, for greasing

90 g/3¼ oz arborio rice

350 ml/12 fl oz milk

3–4 tbsp sugar

½ tsp freshly grated nutmeg

½ tsp salt, plus a pinch

175 g/6 oz plain flour

1½ tsp baking powder

1 tsp bicarbonate of soda

1–2 tbsp caster sugar

1 egg

175 ml/6 fl oz milk

120 ml/4 fl oz soured cream or yogurt

1 tbsp butter, melted

2 tbsp honey

½ tsp almond essence

2 tbsp toasted flaked almonds

icing sugar, for dusting (optional)

MUSCAT BERRIES

450 g/1 lb mixed summer berries, such as strawberries (halved), raspberries and blueberries

1–2 tbsp sugar

50 ml/2 fl oz Muscat wine

1 Put the rice, milk, sugar, nutmeg and ½ teaspoon of salt in a heavy-based saucepan. Bring to the boil, reduce the heat slightly and cook, stirring constantly, until the rice is tender and the milk almost absorbed. Allow to cool.

2 Combine the flour, baking powder, bicarbonate of soda, pinch of salt and the sugar. In a bowl, beat the egg, milk, soured cream, butter, honey and almond essence with an electric mixer until smooth. Gradually beat in the rice. Stir in the flour mixture and the almonds.

3 Gently spoon the mixture into a 23-25 cm/9-10 inch well-greased cake tin with a removable bottom, smoothing the top evenly. Bake the cake in a preheated oven at 160°C/325°F/Gas

MASCARPONE CREAM

2 tbsp Muscat wine

1 tbsp honey

½ tsp almond essence

225 ml/8 fl oz mascarpone cheese

Mark 3 for about 20 minutes until golden. Cool in the tin on a wire rack.

4 Put the berries in a bowl and add the sugar and wine. To make the mascarpone cream, stir all the ingredients together and chill.

5 Remove the sides of the tin and slide the cake on to a serving plate. Dust with icing sugar and serve the Sweet Risotto Cake warm with the Muscat Berries and mascarpone cream (pipe the cream on top of the cake, if you prefer).

Mascarpone Cheesecake

The mascarpone gives this baked cheesecake a wonderfully tangy flavour.
Ricotta cheese could be used as an alternative.

NUTRITIONAL INFORMATION

Calories 327	Sugars 25g
Protein 9g	Fat 18g
Carbohydrate . . .33g	Saturates 11g

30 mins   45 mins

SERVES 8

INGREDIENTS

2 tsp melted butter, for greasing

50 g/1¾ oz unsalted butter

150 g/5½ oz ginger biscuits, crushed

25 g/1 oz stem ginger, chopped

500 g/1 lb 2 oz mascarpone cheese

finely grated rind and juice of 2 lemons

100 g/3½ oz caster sugar

2 large eggs, separated

fruit coulis (see Cook's Tip), to serve

1 Grease and line the base of a 25 cm/10 inch springform cake tin or other loose-bottomed tin.

2 Melt the butter in a pan and stir in the crushed biscuits and chopped ginger. Line the tin with the biscuit mixture, pressing it about 5 mm/¼ inch up the sides.

3 Beat together the cheese, lemon rind and juice, sugar and egg yolks until quite smooth.

4 Whisk the egg whites until they are stiff and fold into the cheese and lemon mixture.

5 Pour the mixture into the prepared tin and bake in a preheated oven, at 180°C/350°F/Gas Mark 4, for 35–45 minutes until just set. It is quite normal if the cake cracks or sinks during the baking process.

6 Leave the cheesecake in the tin to cool. Serve with a spoonful of fruit coulis (see Cook's Tip).

COOK'S TIP

Fruit coulis can be made by cooking 400 g/14 oz fruit, such as blueberries, for 5 minutes with 2 tablespoons of water. Sieve the mixture, then stir in 1 tablespoon (or more to taste) of sieved icing sugar. Leave to cool. before serving.

Crispy-topped Fruit Bake

Crushed sugar cubes add a lovely crunchy texture to this easy fruit pudding containing a tempting combination of blackberries and apple.

NUTRITIONAL INFORMATION

Calories 227	Sugars 30g
Protein 5g	Fat 1g
Carbohydrate . . .53g	Saturates 0.2g

40 mins   45 mins

SERVES 10

INGREDIENTS

2 tsp melted butter, for greasing

350 g/12 oz cooking apples

3 tbsp lemon juice

300 g/10½ oz self-raising wholemeal flour

½ tsp baking powder

1 tsp ground cinnamon, plus extra
  for dusting

175 g/6 oz prepared blackberries, thawed
  if frozen, plus extra to decorate

175 g/6 oz light muscovado sugar

1 medium egg, beaten

200 ml/7 fl oz low-fat natural fromage frais

60 g/2 oz white or brown sugar cubes,
  lightly crushed

sliced eating apple, to decorate

1 Preheat the oven to 190°C/375°F/Gas Mark 5. Grease and line a 900 g/2 lb loaf tin with baking parchment. Core, peel and finely dice the apples. Place them in a saucepan with the lemon juice, bring to the boil, then cover and simmer for 10 minutes until soft and pulpy. Beat well and set aside to cool.

2 Sift the flour, baking powder and 1 tsp cinnamon into a bowl, adding any flour husks that remain in the sieve. Stir in 115 g/4 oz blackberries and all the sugar.

3 Make a well in the centre of the ingredients and add the egg, fromage frais and cooled apple purée. Mix well to incorporate thoroughly. Spoon the mixture into the prepared loaf tin and smooth the top.

4 Sprinkle with the remaining blackberries, pressing them into the cake mixture. Top with crushed sugar lumps. Bake for 40–45 minutes. Leave to cool in the tin.

5 Remove the cake from the tin and peel away the baking parchment. Serve dusted with cinnamon and decorated with extra blackberries and apple slices.

VARIATION

Try replacing the blackberries with blueberries. Use the canned or frozen variety if fresh blueberries are unavailable.

Almond Cheesecakes

These creamy cheese desserts are so delicious that it is hard to believe they are low in fat.

NUTRITIONAL INFORMATION

Calories	.361	Sugars	.29g
Protein	.16g	Fat	.15g
Carbohydrate	.43g	Saturates	.4g

40 mins plus refrigeration time

10 mins

SERVES 4

INGREDIENTS

2 tsp melted butter, for greasing

12 amaretti biscuits

1 egg white, lightly beaten

225 g/8 oz low-fat soft cheese

½ tsp almond essence

½ tsp finely grated lime rind

25 g/1 oz ground almonds

25 g/1 oz caster sugar

60 g/2¼ oz sultanas

2 tsp powdered gelatine

2 tbsp boiling water

2 tbsp lime juice

TO DECORATE

25 g/1 oz toasted flaked almonds

strips of lime rind

1 Preheat the oven to 180°C/350°F/ Gas Mark 4. Place the biscuits in a clean plastic bag, seal the bag and then, using a rolling pin, crush them into small pieces.

2 Place the biscuit crumbs in a separate bowl and bind together with the egg white.

3 Arrange 4 lightly greased non-stick pastry rings or poached egg rings,

9 cm/3½ inches across, on a baking tray lined with baking parchment. Divide the biscuit mixture into 4 equal portions and spoon it into the rings, pressing down well. Bake for 10 minutes until crisp and leave to cool in the rings.

4 Carefully beat together the soft cheese, almond essence, lime rind, ground almonds, sugar and sultanas until they are well mixed.

5 Dissolve the gelatine in the boiling water and stir in the lime juice. Fold into the cheese mixture and spoon over the biscuit bases. Smooth the tops and chill for 1 hour, or until set.

6 Loosen the cheesecakes from the tins using a small palette knife or spatula and transfer to serving plates. Decorate with the toasted flaked almonds and strips of lime rind before serving.

Strawberry Roulade

For a delicious tea-time treat, serve this moist, light sponge rolled up with an almond and strawberry fromage frais filling.

NUTRITIONAL INFORMATION

Calories 166	Sugars 19g
Protein 6g	Fat 3g
Carbohydrate ...30g	Saturates 1g

  45 mins   10 mins

SERVES 8

INGREDIENTS

2 tsp melted butter, for greasing

3 large eggs

125 g/4¼ oz caster sugar

125 g/4¼ oz plain flour

1 tbsp hot water

15 g/½ oz toasted flaked almonds, to decorate

1 tsp icing sugar, to decorate

FILLING

200 ml/7 fl oz low-fat fromage frais

1 tsp almond essence

225 g/8 oz small strawberries

1 Preheat the oven to 220°C/425°F/ Gas Mark 7. Lightly grease a 35 x 25 cm/14 x 10 inch Swiss roll tin and line with baking parchment. Place the eggs in a mixing bowl with the caster sugar. Place the bowl over a pan of hot water and whisk until pale and thick.

2 Remove the bowl from the pan. Sift the flour and fold into the eggs. Add the hot water. Pour the mixture into the tin and bake for 8–10 minutes, until golden and set.

3 Turn the cake out on to a sheet of baking parchment. Peel off the lining paper and roll up the sponge tightly, along with the baking parchment. Wrap in a tea towel and allow to cool.

4 Make the filling. Mix together the fromage frais and the almond essence. Reserving a few strawberries for decoration, wash, hull and slice the remainder. Leave the mixture to chill in the refrigerator until required.

5 Unroll the sponge, spread the fromage frais mixture over it and sprinkle with strawberries. Roll up the sponge again and transfer to a serving plate. Sprinkle with almonds and dust lightly with icing sugar. Decorate with the reserved strawberries.

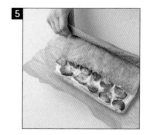

Berry Cheesecake

Use a mixture of berries, such as blueberries, blackberries, raspberries and strawberries, for a really fruity cheesecake.

NUTRITIONAL INFORMATION

Calories	478	Sugars	........28g
Protein	........10g	Fat	.........32g
Carbohydrate	...40g	Saturates	......15g

35 mins plus refrigeration time

0 mins

SERVES 8

INGREDIENTS

BASE

75 g/2¾ oz margarine, plus extra for greasing

175 g/6 oz oatmeal biscuits

50 g/1¾ oz desiccated coconut

FILLING

1½ tsp vegetarian gelatine

9 tbsp cold water

125 ml/4 fl oz evaporated milk

1 egg

6 tbsp soft light brown sugar

450 g/1 lb soft cream cheese

350 g/12 oz mixed berries

2 tbsp clear honey, to top

1 Place the margarine in a saucepan and heat until melted. Put the biscuits in a food processor and process until thoroughly crushed. Alternatively, crush finely with a rolling pin. Stir the biscuit crumbs into the margarine, together with the coconut.

2 Lightly grease a 20 cm/8 inch springform tin and line the base with baking parchment. Press the biscuit mixture evenly into the tin. Set aside in the refrigerator to chill while you prepare the filling for the cheesecake.

3 To make the filling, put the water in a pan and sprinkle the gelatine into it. Stir to dissolve. Bring to the boil and boil for 2 minutes. Leave to cool slightly.

4 Put the milk, egg, sugar and soft cream cheese in a bowl and beat until smooth. Stir in 50 g/1¾ oz of the berries. Add the gelatine in a stream, stirring constantly.

5 Spread the mixture on the biscuit base and return to the refrigerator to chill for 2 hours, or until set.

6 Remove the Berry Cheesecake from the tin and transfer it to a large serving plate. Arrange the remaining berries on top of the cheesecake and drizzle the honey over the top. Serve straight away.

Chocolate Cheesecake

This cheesecake takes a little time to prepare and cook, but is well worth the effort. It is quite rich and is good served with a little fresh fruit.

NUTRITIONAL INFORMATION

Calories 471	Sugars 20g
Protein 10g	Fat 33g
Carbohydrate ...28g	Saturates 5g

20 mins, plus refrigeration time

1¼ hours

SERVES 12

INGREDIENTS

100 g/3½ oz plain flour

100 g/3½ oz almonds, ground

200 g/7 oz demerara sugar

150 g/5½ oz margarine, plus extra for greasing

700 g/1lb 9oz firm tofu

175 ml/6 fl oz vegetable oil

125 ml/4 fl oz orange juice

175 ml/6 fl oz brandy

50 g/1¾ oz cocoa powder, plus extra to decorate

2 tsp almond essence

icing sugar and Cape gooseberries, to decorate

1 Put the flour, ground almonds and 1 tablespoon of the sugar in a bowl and mix well. Rub the margarine into the mixture to form a dough.

2 Lightly grease a 23 cm/9 inch springform tin and line the base with baking parchment. Press the dough into the base of the tin to cover, pushing it right up to the edge.

3 Roughly chop the tofu and put in a food processor with the vegetable oil, orange juice, brandy, cocoa powder, almond essence and remaining sugar and process until smooth and creamy. Pour over the cheesecake base and cook in a preheated oven, at 160°C/325°F/Gas Mark 3, for 1–1¼ hours, or until set.

4 Leave to cool in the tin for 5 minutes, then remove from the tin and chill in the refrigerator. Dust with icing sugar and cocoa powder. Decorate with Cape gooseberries and serve.

COOK'S TIP

Cape gooseberries make an attractive decoration for many desserts. Peel open the papery husks to expose the bright orange fruits.

Lime Cheesecakes

These cheesecakes are flavoured with lime and mint, and set on a base of crushed digestive biscuits mixed with chocolate.

NUTRITIONAL INFORMATION

Calories	696	Sugars 44g
Protein	........18g	Fat 40g
Carbohydrate	...70g	Saturates 22g

30 mins, plus refrigeration time   0 mins

SERVES 2

I N G R E D I E N T S

BASE

25 g/1 oz butter, plus extra for greasing

25 g/1 oz dark chocolate

90 g/3 oz digestive biscuits, crushed

FILLING

finely grated rind of 1 lemon

90 g/3 oz curd cheese

90 g/3 oz low-fat soft cheese

1 mint sprig, chopped very finely (optional)

1 tsp vegetarian gelatine

1 tbsp lime juice

1 egg yolk

40 g/1½ oz caster sugar

TO DECORATE

whipped cream

kiwi fruit slices

mint sprigs

1 Grease 2 fluted, preferably loose-based, 12 cm/4½ inch flan tins thoroughly. To make the base, melt the butter and chocolate in a heatproof bowl over a pan of gently simmering water, or melt in a microwave set on high power for about 1 minute. Stir until smooth.

2 Stir the crushed biscuits evenly through the melted chocolate and then press into the bases of the flan tins, levelling the surface. Chill until set.

3 To make the filling, put the grated lime rind and cheeses into a bowl and beat until smooth and evenly blended. Beat in the mint, if using.

4 Dissolve the gelatine in the lime juice in a heatproof bowl over a pan of simmering water or in a microwave oven set on high power for about 30 seconds.

5 Beat the egg yolk and sugar together until creamy and fold into the cheese mixture, followed by the dissolved gelatine. Pour over the base and chill until set.

6 To serve, remove the cheesecakes carefully from the flan tins. Decorate with whipped cream, slices of kiwi fruit and mint sprigs.

Upside-down Cake

This recipe shows how a classic favourite can be adapted for vegans by using vegetarian margarine and oil instead of butter and eggs.

NUTRITIONAL INFORMATION

Calories 354	Sugars 31g
Protein 3g	Fat 15g
Carbohydrate . . .56g	Saturates 2g

 30 mins   40 mins

SERVES 6

INGREDIENTS

50 g/1¾ oz vegan margarine (cut into small pieces), plus extra for greasing

425 g/15 oz unsweetened canned pineapple pieces, drained and juice reserved

4 tsp cornflour

50 g/1¾ oz soft light brown sugar

125 ml/4 fl oz water

SPONGE

50 ml/2 fl oz sunflower oil

75 g/2¾ oz soft light brown sugar

150 ml/5 fl oz water

150 g/5½ oz plain flour

2 tsp baking powder

1 tsp ground cinnamon

grated rind of 1 lemon

1 Lightly grease a deep 18 cm/7 inch cake tin. To make the pineapple syrup, add the reserved juice from the canned pineapple to the cornflour and mix until it forms a smooth paste. Place the paste in a saucepan along with the sugar, margarine and 125 ml/4 fl oz water, and stir the mixture over a low heat until the sugar has dissolved. Bring to the boil and simmer for 2–3 minutes, until thickened. Set aside to cool slightly.

2 To make the sponge, place the oil, sugar and 150 ml/5 fl oz water in a saucepan. Heat gently until the sugar has dissolved; do not allow it to boil. Remove from the heat and leave to cool. Sieve the flour, baking powder and ground cinnamon into a mixing bowl. Pour the cooled sugar syrup in and beat well.

3 Place the pineapple pieces and lemon rind on the base of the prepared tin and pour over 4 tablespoons of the pineapple syrup. Spoon the sponge mixture on top.

4 Bake in a preheated oven, 180°C/350°F/Gas Mark 4, for 35–40 minutes, until set and a fine metal skewer inserted into the centre comes out clean. Invert on to a plate, leave to stand for 5 minutes, then remove the tin. Serve with the remaining syrup.

Raspberry Shortcake

For this lovely summery dessert, two crisp rounds of shortbread are sandwiched together with fresh raspberries and lightly whipped cream.

NUTRITIONAL INFORMATION

Calories . . . . . . .496 Sugars 14g
Protein . . . . .4g Fat 41g
Carbohydrate . . .30g Saturates 26g

15 mins   15 mins

SERVES 8

I N G R E D I E N T S

100 g/3½ oz butter (cut into cubes), plus extra for greasing

175 g/6 oz self-raising flour

75 g/2¾ oz caster sugar

1 egg yolk

1 tbsp rose water

600 ml/1 pint whipping cream, lightly whipped

225 g/8 oz raspberries, plus a few extra for decoration

TO DECORATE

icing sugar

mint leaves

1 Lightly grease 2 baking trays with a little butter.

2 To make the shortcake, sieve the flour into a bowl. Rub the butter into the flour with your fingers until the mixture resembles breadcrumbs.

3 Stir the sugar, egg yolk and rose water into the mixture, and with your fingers, form a soft dough. Divide the dough into two equal portions.

4 On a lightly floured surface, roll each piece of dough into a 20 cm/ 8 inch round. Carefully lift each one with the rolling pin and put on to one of the prepared baking trays. Crimp the edges of the dough.

5 Bake in a preheated oven, at 190°C/ 375°F/Gas Mark 5, for 15 minutes until lightly golden. Transfer the shortcakes to a wire rack and leave to cool completely.

6 Mix the whipped cream with the raspberries and spoon the mixture on top of one of the shortcakes, spreading it out evenly. Top with the other shortcake round, dust with a little icing sugar and decorate with the extra raspberries and mint leaves.

COOK'S TIP

The shortcake can be made a few days in advance and stored in an airtight container until required.

Pavlova

This delicious dessert originated in Australia. Serve it with sharp fruits to balance the sweetness of the meringue.

NUTRITIONAL INFORMATION

Calories 354   Sugars 34g
Protein ....3g   Fat 24g
Carbohydrate ...34g   Saturates 15g

   25 mins   1¼ hours

MAKES 6

I N G R E D I E N T S

2 tsp melted butter, for greasing

3 egg whites

pinch of salt

175 g/6 oz caster sugar

300 ml/10 fl oz double cream, lightly whipped

fresh fruit of your choice (raspberries, strawberries, peaches, passion fruit or Cape gooseberries

1 Lightly grease and line a baking sheet with a sheet of baking parchment.

2 Whisk the egg whites and a pinch of salt in a large bowl, until they form soft peaks.

3 Whisk in the sugar, a little at a time, whisking well after each addition. Continue the process until all the sugar has been incorporated.

4 Spoon three-quarters of the mixture on to the baking sheet, forming a circle 20 cm/8 inches in diameter.

5 Place spoonfuls of the remaining meringue around the edge of the circle so they join up to make a rim, creating a nest shape.

6 Bake in a preheated oven, 140°C/ 275°F/Gas Mark 1, for 1¼ hours.

7 Turn the heat off, but leave the Pavlova in the oven until it is completely cold.

8 To serve, place the Pavlova on a serving dish. Spread with the whipped cream, then arrange the fresh fruit on top. Do not decorate the Pavlova too far in advance or it will go soggy.

 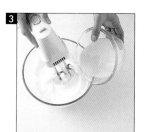 

COOK'S TIP

If you are worried about making the circular meringue, draw a circle on the baking parchment, turn it over, then spoon the meringue inside the outline.

Baked Cheesecake

This cheesecake has a rich creamy texture, but contains no dairy produce being made with tofu instead. It is served with mango sauce.

NUTRITIONAL INFORMATION

Calories	....	.282
Protein	....	.9g
Carbohydrate	...	29g

Sugars	....	17g
Fat	....	15g
Saturates	....	.4g

35 mins, plus refrigeration time   40 mins

SERVES 6

INGREDIENTS

125 g/4¼ oz digestive biscuits, crushed

50 g/1¾ oz margarine, melted, plus extra for greasing

50 g/1¾ oz stoned dates, chopped

4 tbsp lemon juice

grated rind of 1 lemon

3 tbsp water

350 g/12 oz firm tofu

150 ml/5 fl oz apple juice

1 banana, mashed

1 tsp vanilla essence

1 mango, peeled and chopped

1 Lightly grease a round 18 cm/7 inch cake tin with a loose base.

2 Mix together the digestive biscuit crumbs and melted margarine in a bowl. Press the mixture into the base of the prepared tin.

3 Put the chopped dates, lemon juice, lemon rind and water into a saucepan and bring to the boil. Simmer for 5 minutes until the dates are soft, then mash them roughly with a fork.

4 Place the mixture in a food processor with the tofu, apple juice, mashed banana and vanilla essence. Process until the mixture is a thick, smooth purée.

5 Carefully pour the tofu purée on to the prepared biscuit crumb base.

6 Bake in a preheated oven, 180°C/350°F/Gas Mark 4, for 30–40 minutes, until lightly golden. Leave to cool in the tin, then chill thoroughly before serving.

7 Place the chopped mango in a food processor and process until a smooth sauce. Serve the mango sauce with the cheesecake.

Apple Cake with Cider

This can be eaten as a cake at tea time or with a cup of coffee, or it can be warmed through and served with cream for a dessert.

NUTRITIONAL INFORMATION

Calories 263	Sugars 22g
Protein 4g	Fat 9g
Carbohydrate ...43g	Saturates 5g

🍰 🍰 🍰

🍲 25 mins   🕐 40 mins

SERVES 8

I N G R E D I E N T S

75 g/2¾ oz butter (cut into small pieces), plus extra for greasing

225 g/8 oz self-raising flour

1 tsp baking powder

75 g/2¾ oz caster sugar

50 g/1¾ oz dried apple, chopped

75 g/2¾ oz raisins

150 ml/5 fl oz sweet cider

1 egg, beaten

175 g/6 oz raspberries

1 Grease a 20 cm/8 inch cake tin and line with baking parchment.

2 Sieve the flour and baking powder into a mixing bowl and rub in the butter with your fingertips until the mixture resembles fine breadcrumbs.

3 Stir in the caster sugar, chopped dried apple and raisins.

4 Add the sweet cider and egg. Mix together all the ingredients until thoroughly blended. Very gently stir in the raspberries so they do not break up.

5 Pour the mixture into the prepared cake tin.

6 Bake in a preheated oven, 190°C/375°F/Gas Mark 5, for about 40 minutes until risen and lightly golden.

7 Leave the cake to cool in the tin, then turn out on to a wire rack. Leave until completely cold before serving.

VARIATION

If you do not want to use cider, replace it with clear apple juice, if you prefer.

Almond Cake

A honey syrup glaze is applied to this cake as soon as it leaves the oven and seeps through as it cools, keeping the cake moist.

NUTRITIONAL INFORMATION

Calories 324	Sugars 27g
Protein 5g	Fat 16g
Carbohydrate ...43g	Saturates 4g

25 mins   50 mins

SERVES 8

INGREDIENTS

100 g/3½ oz soft margarine, plus extra
   for greasing

50 g/1¾ oz soft light brown sugar

2 eggs

175 g/6 oz self-raising flour

1 tsp baking powder

4 tbsp milk

2 tbsp clear honey

50 g/1¾ oz flaked almonds

SYRUP

150 ml/5 fl oz clear honey

2 tbsp lemon juice

1 Grease a round 18 cm/7 inch cake tin and line with baking parchment.

2 Place the margarine, brown sugar, eggs, flour, baking powder, milk and honey in a large mixing bowl and beat well with a wooden spoon for about 1 minute until all the ingredients are thoroughly mixed together.

3 Spoon into the prepared tin, level the surface with a spoon or a knife, and sprinkle with the almonds.

4 Bake the cake in a preheated oven, 180°C/350°F/Gas Mark 4, for about 50 minutes or until the cake is well risen and a fine skewer inserted into the centre comes out clean.

5 Meanwhile, make the syrup. Combine the honey and lemon juice in a small saucepan and simmer for about 5 minutes or until the syrup starts to coat the back of a spoon.

6 As soon as the cake comes out of the oven, pour the syrup over it, allowing it to seep into the middle of the cake.

7 Leave the cake to cool for at least 2 hours before slicing.

COOK'S TIP

Experiment with different flavoured honeys for the syrup glaze until you find one that you think tastes best.

Chocolate Coconut Roulade

Here, a coconut-flavoured roulade is encased in a rich chocolate coating.
It is served with fresh raspberry coulis, which provides a piquant contrast.

NUTRITIONAL INFORMATION

Calories 299	Sugars 36g
Protein 4g	Fat 15g
Carbohydrate . . .40g	Saturates 9g

40 mins 12 mins

SERVES 8

INGREDIENTS

3 eggs

75 g/2¾ oz caster sugar, plus extra

50 g/1¾ oz self-raising flour

1 tbsp block creamed coconut, softened
    with 1 tbsp boiling water

25 g/1 oz desiccated coconut

6 tbsp good-quality raspberry conserve

CHOCOLATE COATING

200 g/7 oz dark chocolate

5 tbsp butter

2 tbsp golden syrup

RASPBERRY COULIS

225 g/8 oz fresh or frozen raspberries
    (defrosted if frozen)

2 tbsp water

4 tbsp icing sugar

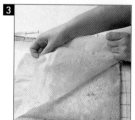

1 Grease and line a 23 x 30 cm/9 x 12 inch Swiss roll tin with baking parchment. Whisk the eggs and caster sugar in a large mixing bowl (with a hand or electric whisk) for about 10 minutes, or until the mixture is very light and foamy and the whisk leaves a trail that lasts a few seconds when the whisk is lifted.

2 Sieve the flour and fold in with a metal spoon or a spatula. Fold in the creamed coconut and desiccated coconut.

Pour the mixture into the prepared tin and bake in a preheated oven, 200°C/400°F/ Gas Mark 6, for 10–12 minutes or until springy to the touch.

3 Sprinkle a sheet of baking parchment with a little caster sugar and place on top of a damp tea towel. Turn the cake out on to the parchment and carefully peel away the lining paper. Spread the jam over the sponge and roll up from the short end, using the tea towel to help you. Place

seam-side down on a wire rack and leave to cool completely.

4 Meanwhile, make the coating. Melt the chocolate and butter, stirring. Stir in the golden syrup; leave to cool for 5 minutes. Spread it over the cooled roulade and leave to set. To make the coulis, purée the fruit in a food processor with the water and sugar; sieve to remove the seeds. Cut the roulade into slices and serve with the raspberry coulis.

Chocolate Rum Babas

A little bit fiddly to make, but well worth the effort. Indulge in these tasty cakes with coffee, or serve them as a dessert with summer fruits.

NUTRITIONAL INFORMATION

Calories	388	Sugars	........40g
Protein	.........5g	Fat	..........17g
Carbohydrate	...57g	Saturates	.......2g

40 mins, plus rising time   15 mins

SERVES 4

I N G R E D I E N T S

2 tsp melted butter, for greasing

100 g/3½ oz strong plain flour

2 tbsp cocoa powder

5 g/⅛ oz sachet easy-blend dried yeast

pinch of salt

1 tbsp caster sugar

40 g/1½ oz dark chocolate, grated

2 eggs

3 tbsp milk (tepid)

4 tbsp butter, melted

S Y R U P

4 tbsp clear honey

2 tbsp water

4 tbsp rum

T O   S E R V E

whipped cream

cocoa powder, to dust

fresh fruit, optional

1 Lightly grease 4 individual ring tins. In a large warmed mixing bowl, sieve the flour and cocoa powder together. Stir in the yeast, salt, sugar and chocolate. In a separate bowl, beat the eggs, add the milk and butter, and beat until mixed.

2 Make a well in the centre of the dry ingredients and pour in the egg mixture, beating to mix to a batter. Beat the mixture thoroughly for 10 minutes, ideally in a food processor with a dough hook. Divide the mixture between the tins – it should come halfway up the sides of the tins.

3 Place on a baking tray and cover with a damp tea towel. Leave in a warm place until the mixture rises almost to the tops of the tins. Bake in a preheated oven, 200°C/400°F/Gas Mark 6, for 15 minutes.

4 To make the syrup, gently heat all of the ingredients in a small pan. Turn out the babas and put on a wire rack placed above a tray to catch the syrup. Drizzle the syrup over the babas and leave for at least 2 hours for the syrup to soak in. Once or twice, spoon the syrup that has collected in the tray over the babas.

5 Fill the centre of the babas with whipped cream and sprinkle a little cocoa powder over the top. Serve the babas with fresh fruit, if desired.

NOTE

This book uses metric and imperial measurements. Follow the same units
of measurement throughout; do not mix metric and imperial.
All spoon measurements are level: teaspoons are assumed to be 5 ml, and
tablespoons are assumed to be 15 ml. Unless otherwise stated,
milk is assumed to be full fat, eggs and individual vegetables such as potatoes
are medium, and pepper is freshly ground black pepper.

The nutritional information provided for each recipe is per serving or per person.
Optional ingredients, variations or serving suggestions have
not been included in the calculations. The times given for each recipe are an approximate
guide only because the preparation times may differ according to the techniques used by
different people and the cooking times may vary as a result of the type of oven used.

Recipes using raw or very lightly cooked eggs should be
avoided by infants, the elderly, pregnant women, convalescents,
and anyone suffering from an illness.

The publisher would like to thank
Steamer Trading Cookshop, Lewes, East Sussex, for the kind loan of props.